*This book is dedicated
to my wife Christine
and thousands of other
Christians who like her
have dedicated
their lives to seeing
God's kingdom come among
the poor and marginalized
of our world.*

Live it up!

HOW TO CREATE A LIFE YOU CAN LOVE

TOM SINE

Foreword by Tony Campolo

HERALD PRESS
Scottdale, Pennsylvania
Waterloo, Ontario

Library of Congress Cataloging-in-Publication Data
Sine, Tom.
    [Why settle for more and miss the best?]
    Live it up! : creating a life you can love / Tom Sine : foreword
by Tony Campolo.
        p. cm.
    Rev. ed. of: Why settle for more and miss the best? 1st ed. c1987.
    Includes bibliographical references.
    ISBN 0-8361-3629-2 (alk. paper)
    1. Christian life—1960- I. Title.
BV4501.2.S47254 1993
248.4—dc20   93-32174
                                                                  CIP

The paper used in this publication is recycled and meets the minimum re-
quirements of American National Standard for Information Sciences—
Permanence of Paper for Printed Library Materials, ANSI Z39.48-1984.

All Bible quotations are used by permission, all rights reserved, and unless
otherwise indicated are from *The King James Version of the Bible*; NIV, *The Holy
Bible, New International Version*, copyright © 1973, 1978, 1984 International
Bible Society, Zondervan Bible Publishers; NASB, the *New American Standard
Bible*, © The Lockman Foundation 1960, 1962, 1963, 1968, 1971, 1972, 1973,
1975; RSV, *The Revised Standard Version of the Bible*, copyrighted 1946, 1952, ©
1971, 1973 by the Division of Christian Education of the National Council of
the Churches of Christ in the USA; PHILLIPS, *The New Testament in Modern
English* by J. B. Phillips, published by The Macmillan Company, © 1958, 1960,
1972 by J. B. Phillips.

LIVE IT UP!
Copyright © 1993 by Herald Press, Scottdale, Pa. 15683
    Published simultaneously in Canada by Herald Press,
    Waterloo, Ont. N2L 6H7. All rights reserved
First edition published under the title, *Why Settle for
More and Miss the Best?* (Word Books, 1987).
Library of Congress Catalog Number: 93-32174
International Standard Book Number: 0-8361-3629-2
Printed in the United States of America
Book and cover design by Merrill R. Miller; "Link" drawings by Tom Sine

1 2 3 4 5 6 7 8 9 10 00 99 98 97 96 95 94 93

Contents

Foreword by Tony Campolo   7
Acknowledgments   10

Start Here   11

   Introducing Link   16
1. Discovering Life   19
2. Discerning Half-truths and False Visions   34
3. Connecting with the Story of God   67
4. Remembering Stories of Hope   94
5. Choosing a Life That Counts   113
6. Discovering a Life You Can Love   133
7. Sharing Life Beyond the Doors of Home and Church   161
8. Creating New Possibilities   185

Begin Now   206

A Guide for Study and Action   213
Notes   226
The Author   231

Foreword

Subconsciously, I always believed that the Sermon on the Mount was not meant for ordinary Christians. It seemed to me that the teachings set forth by Jesus in Matthew 5, 6, and 7 were okay for the Mother Teresa's of the world. But the rest of us couldn't be expected to live out these commands.

The Beatitudes set forth by Jesus in Matthew 5 seem opposed to what the dominant culture has prescribed as a normal, happy lifestyle. Jesus says, "Blessed are the poor"—or, as Dietrich Bonhoeffer suggests, blessed are those who have become poor as they have responded to the needs of the poor and the oppressed. We have been brought up to believe that the wealthy are the happy people.

Jesus tells us that people who cry because their hearts are broken over the things that break God's heart are the fulfilled people of this world. We have been trained to believe that fulfillment comes to those who make their lives an endless round of partygoing with plenty of laughs.

The "will to power" is viewed as a positive personality trait in a competitive world in which only the fittest survive. But Jesus tells us that the meek are the blessed.

In our attempts to bolster law and order, we believe capital punishment is an essential deterrent to crime. Consequently Jesus' call to be merciful seems like unrealistic softness.

We have come to accept national policies which are designed to further our economic self-interests, even when such policies require that we bolster the regimes of totalitarian dictators. Contrary to such policies, we read that Jesus blesses those who hunger and thirst for righteousness. To those of us who have come to believe that social ethics are complex if not paradoxical in nature, Jesus declares that those who live with pure hearts and accept truth in its simplicity are the ones who will see God.

In a world arena where the accepted logic is that the only way to prevent war is to prepare for it, Jesus calls us to be peacemakers. Such a lifestyle sets us up to be persecuted and reviled, and makes us vulnerable to those who would "do all manner of evil against." Yet Jesus says that if such consequences come from our radical commitment to his values, we should rejoice.

It is no surprise that Christianity has taken the values prescribed by Jesus and inverted them. It should shock no one that the church restates the message of the Master so that it often comes out meaning just the opposite of what the Lord intended. For the sophisticated members of the world's intelligentsia, the Sermon on the Mount seems foolishly naive.

Then there are those like Tom Sine who are not so convinced that the wisdom of this world is all that wise. He and other aliens in this strange and distant land called North America probingly ask whether those who have followed the "reasonable" ways of the world have ended up happy.

Sine and his friends are quick to ask if the wealthy have really found a way to happiness and if the pot of emotional riches lies waiting to be found at the end of the corporate rainbow. They sense a lack of joy among those down-to-earth, realistic executive-types who have bought into the American dream. They discern an absence of joy among the children who live in the affluence their parents have provided.

Sine and his counterculture associates contend that what Jesus taught two thousand years ago in the Sermon on the Mount is a viable lifestyle that will produce joy and personal ecstasy in the midst of modern North America. Those voices crying in the wilderness call people to abandon the temptation to live in pursuit of the reasonable goals prescribed by the dominant culture. The voices call instead for all of us to seek vocations wherein we can be instruments for propagating the values of another kingdom, the kingdom of God.

This book is a call to abandon the comfortable, pleasant, attractive, reasonable form of slavery that has come to typify so many of our lives. It is a call to recognize that the foolishness of the gospel is more reasonable in the end than the wisdom of this world. *Live It Up!* offers help for those who have begun to doubt the validity of conventional values and are looking for a better way to find joy and meaning in life.

—*Tony Campolo*
St. Davids, Pennsylvania

Acknowledgments

This book was conceived at a conference on the nature and mission of the church. At the conclusion of the conference, leaders from different countries expressed a desire to present in more popular form the scholarly insights derived from our biblical study. The result was *Live It Up!* This book, therefore, is offered with gratitude to the hundreds of sisters and brothers from all over the world who participated in this important convocation.

I am particularly grateful to those who assisted me in editing this revised manuscript including my wife Christine, Eydie Coursy and Michael King from Herald Press. Of course I couldn't have completed this task without the support of my mother, my two sons and the support, prayers, and encouragement of my small group and many friends. Finally, I feel a greater sense of indebtedness to all who have gone before us in the story of God, particularly those who participated in the Celtic Christian movement in the sixth through the tenth centuries.

—*Tom Sine*
Seattle, Washington

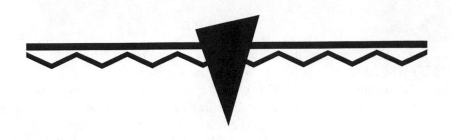

Start Here

U P?
  Live it up?
  What's up?
Now there's a question!

Many of us seem to be working very hard at living it up—yet we seem to spend a lot of time feeling down. Is that your story? Is life getting you down? Are you confused about what's up?

Everywhere I go, I meet people whose lives are busier and more frenetic than ever before. But they no longer seem to have any idea of how to live it up.

Frank and Jenny celebrated hitting their mid-forties by taking the plunge. They bought a Winnebago camper and a Chris-craft power boat. As they brought their purchases home, Frank and Jenny were higher than a kite.

Early that first Saturday morning they headed for Lake Michigan towing their power boat behind their shiny new camper. They spent the whole Memorial Day weekend with their two junior high kids, living it up.

The moment Frank and Jenny returned home, they began to face the cost this approach to living it up would require. To make the payments on their expensive new toys as well as maintain their existing house and car payments, they would both need to take extra part-time jobs.

Early one morning three years later, Jenny and Frank woke up exhausted and ill. They called in sick to their weekend jobs and spent the morning in bed talking about their lives and why they were feeling so low. They had both been working 60 hours a week for three years trying to get a piece of the good life and live up to other peoples' expectations. Belatedly they were discovering how little time they had left over for their kids, one another, or their church. They were in pit-city.

Incredibly, since that first glorious weekend three years earlier, they only had their camper and boat out of the driveway twice. They began asking if there wasn't something terribly self-defeating about killing themselves to make payments on something they rarely had time to use. How, they wondered, could they have gotten so far down by working so hard to live it up.

Mark and Celia were young adults who hadn't started their families yet. Like Frank and Jenny they found themselves caught in time-stressed lifestyles. They too were working extra jobs—but not to purchase a boat and camper or even a house. They were struggling just to stay even. They were depressed because they could see no end in sight, no way up.

Julie was a recent college grad. She had assumed that after college life would be less pressured and more fun. Like so many grads these days, Julie had no direction for her life. In response to her budget crunch of accumulated bills and college loans she took the first job she could find after graduation—selling clothes in the basement of Nordstroms in Seattle and she hated it. Like the others, Julie had no idea of what's up or how to get there either.

In my travels I run into many good people. They are trying to do what's best for their families. They try to be active at church, to be responsible at work, to enjoy life. But something is wrong. They started out confident they knew how to live it up—only to discover life was getting them down.

Know the feeling? Rushing! Running! Ripping around. From the first bell to the final test pattern, life for too many of us is just one frantic dash after another. Fully 89 percent of American adults—nearly 160 million people—say they are chronically stressed out. Sixty four million report that they suffer regularly from stress and are doing nothing about it.[1]

Is there anything beyond the stress race? Does God have a purpose for us other than our burning out in the fast lane?

Absolutely! God not only wants to help us catch an easier rhythm. God longs to fill our lives with direction, purpose, and celebration. The Creator God invites us to a new way up. God invites us to be much more fully part of a story that is literally changing the world. And as we become more a part of God's story we will find a more festive way of life than ever imagined.

Do you want to find a way of life more satisfying and fulfilling than anything the stress-race can offer . . . that makes a little difference in the world? Then keep reading!

The sole purpose of this book is to enable you to discover a new way to live it up and create a life you can love!

How do we find a new way up? We begin by trying to figure out what has brought us down.

The problem for many of us is not knowing what we're here for. In a book of Hasidic tales, Elie Weisel tells of a rabbi who maintained a lifelong ritual. Every week he went to a special place in the forest near his home. He lit a fire and said a prayer that recalled the story of the salvation of God.

Impressed by the old man, the Rabbi's students continued his ritual after his death. However, little by little they changed their tradition. First they lost the sacred place in the forest. Then they failed to light the fire. Finally they forgot to pray. Eventually all they could do was recite the story of the salvation of God.

The opposite seems to have happened among North American Christians. We haven't forgotten our rituals. We still pray. But we are forgetting our story. And without a clear sense of the story of God, we are settling for other stories which can't tell us how to truly live it up.

In this book we will take a close look at the stories we have embraced and the story we have misplaced. I believe that only as we recover something of *the* story and purposes of the God who created us do we have any hope of finding a new way up . . . a way of life we will genuinely love.

Whether we recognize it or not, the Creator is intimately a part of all our lives and stories. God is with us at the birth of a child, the reunion of a family, and the quiet moments of every day. God is also there when the bottom falls away and our lives seem shipwrecked. But we have to choose if we want to be a part of God's story and devote our lives to God's purposes.

As I point out in *Wild Hope*,[2] we are not only living at the threshold time of the last decade of the twentieth century and the third millennium since the coming of Christ. We are also living in a world changing at blinding speed.

That means our futures will likely be filled with an avalanche of change. For many, those coming waves of change will be overwhelming and will significantly increase the stress beyond which we can cope. Only those of us with a compelling sense of purpose will live effectively and creatively in such a world.

Many of us found that sense of compelling direction by linking our lives to the purposes of the God who created us, who promises to make "all things new." And God is beginning to transform our entire lives. I don't think it is any accident that we are living in the final days of the twentieth century. I believe God has called us onto the stage for such a time as this.

God isn't looking for luminaries—the prestigious and the powerful—to advance God's cause. As I suggest in the *Mustard Seed Conspiracy*,[3] the Creator God has chosen to work through your life and mine to advance God's loving purposes in the world. It is through ordinary people, through the insignificant and imperfect, that God conspires to make a world new.

Donald Kraybill is right. In his classic, *The Upside-Down Kingdom*,[4] he points out that only as we come down from all the false stories and self-involved aspirations do we have any hope of finding a new way up—a way of life in which the last are first, losers are winners, and dying is living.

A Look Ahead

To journey together toward a new way up, we need a road map. In chapter 1 we will spend more time trying to understand what has brought us down. In chapter 2 we will analyze the false stories and failed purposes to which many of us have given our lives. The launch pad of the book is chapter 3. Here we will try to travel through the entire sweep of the story of God with a single goal—finding a new way up.

The story of God doesn't end with the book of Acts. So in chapter 4 we will visit a few scenes of the ongoing saga of God's people who choose to put God's purposes first in their lives.

You and I come onstage in chapter 5. Here we will consider placing God's purposes first in our lives and beginning a new journey up. In chapter 6 we will learn specific new ways to become the presence of God's new order. In chapter 7 we will explore innovative ways churches can put first things first.

This entire book is about creativity—how you create a life you can love. Therefore the final chapter shows how to create imaginative new possibilities for your life and family in innovative timestyles, cooperative housing, alternative celebrations, and ministries. Your greatest untapped resource in finding a new way up is your own imagination.

Live It Up! is designed for use in adult study groups as well as a college or seminary textbook. Questions are included at the end of each chapter to assist in class discussion. A visual summary called "Lifelinks" follows the questions and emphasizes the central thrust of that chapter.

You are invited to join us on a journey to discover a way of life that is more fulfilling, satisfying, and festive than anything the rat race can offer.

You are invited to create a life you can really love.

FOR THOUGHT AND DISCUSSION

As we begin this journey together, ponder these questions:

1. What pressures are making your life frantic?
2. In what specific ways have you tried to "live it up"?
3. What is your sense of God's call on your life? How have you responded to that call?

LIFE LINKS

Welcome to
Live it up!
How to Create a Life You Can Love

introducing link

I've discovered in both my writing and speaking that I am not always as clear as I would like to be. For that reason I have asked for some help from a friend. I would like to introduce you to my friend, Link.

Any similarity to my other friend, Tony Campolo, who generously did the foreword for this book, is purely coincidental. Link has never taught sociology, worn glasses, or "sprays" when he speaks. And you will notice, that unlike

Tony, Link has a bit of hair.

But Link is given to definite opinions.

At the end of each chapter he will join us and explain what I was really trying to say. Usually he will answer three questions:

1. What are our life directions?

2. How are we connected to those life directions?

3. What are likely to be the consequences of following different life directions?

I think you will find Link a very agreeable companion on your journey through this book. I hope he will make the thrust of each chapter a bit clearer.

Discovering Life

Life! this book is about life . . . about having the time of your life. It's about those who have discovered the secret of living life fully and festively—and about those who are missing it.

Do you ever long to live more deeply, more significantly, and more joyfully—to feel your life counts? In this chapter we will take a candid look at the lives we are leading and the mountains we are scaling. Then we will introduce the possibility of climbing a different mountain . . . to find a new way up.

The purpose of this chapter, therefore, is to explore why our lives are so incredibly stressed yet so lacking in direction, purpose, and celebration. To get us started, let me share a quick story about someone who gave chaotic living a whole new meaning.

A publisher in Britain wanting to curry favor asked if I would like to go on a tour of London while there. Being a convinced anglophile, I jumped at the opportunity.

The publisher sent a chap named Bryan to take me on the tour. That day turned out to be one of the more remarkable ones of my entire life—all because of Bryan.

Bryan was a thoroughly likable fellow. But in his efforts to get to the top he had lost an executive position in advertising, been divorced, and gone bankrupt. He was struggling to start over again at age thirty-five.

We met in the coffee shop of an expensive downtown hotel. Bryan sat down across from me in the booth, quickly crossed his legs—and went screaming under the table. Somehow in the relatively simple task of crossing his legs he had virtually shattered his kneecap.

Fifteen minutes later we were leaving the hotel. I heard screams behind me. There was Bryan with his finger caught in the top of the revolving door . . . going around and around and around.

I am not exaggerating—every fifteen minutes a new disaster befell Bryan. I kept saying to myself "What's going on? Are we on Candid Camera?"

After a series of calamities, I developed a theory of "self-victimization," only to have my theory destroyed moments later at lunch. Since it was a beautiful blue sky, we decided to eat out of doors on Carnaby Street. Bryan wanted a baked potato, so he joined a long line leading to a street vendor. After what seemed forever, he brought the potato back to the table, peeled back the foil, cut the potato open, and took a bite. It was ice-cold. Bryan didn't care. He hadn't had breakfast, he hadn't had a good day, and he was famished.

As he was on approach for bite number two, out of nowhere a seagull came. It hit the baked potato dead center. By this time I was praying for Bryan, "Lord, have mercy! Spare him! Spare him!"

Boarding the subway back to his office at the end of this remarkable day, I thought, *Thank God nothing can happen to Bryan now*. Wrong! Bryan sat down with a metal panel on his left side. About six inches to his right was a large, burly guy who looked like a coal miner. There were empty seats all over the subway. And I was sitting across from Bryan.

At the next stop a woman got on. A huge woman. She wasn't interested in any of the empty seats. She wanted the six inches next to Bryan. She brought it on back and it looked like someone jammed Bryan in a garbage compacter. The remaining 45 minute subway ride Bryan endured in evident pain.

As we got off the subway Bryan said, "Tom, you may not believe this, but last week I was actually hit by an ambulance."

"Bryan," I said, "I have no trouble believing that at all!"

In our mad scramble to live it up, many of us spend much more time in garbage compactors and on the front ends of ambulances than we need to—often because we are confused about what's up. We urgently need to clear up our confusion about what's up and how to get there.

Movin' on Up

"King of the Mountain" was a popular game when I was a kid. I remember struggling to the top of a huge mountain of dirt, only to have a big guy at the top send me hurtling down to the bottom again. Spitting dirt, I would begin my climb all over again—and quickly discover a new way down.

On one of those repeated ascents, exhausted and caked with dirt, I got stuck halfway up. I can still see myself on the side of the hill, my friends climbing over me and using my skinny body for a ladder (we really knew how to have fun in those days).

In recent years, I have met many people for whom "King of the Mountain" is no kid's game. They are absolutely exhausted from their strenuous efforts to make it to the top in their careers, the 'burbs, and in the eyes of their friends and family. They often pay a high cost regardless of whether they make it to the top, get stuck halfway up, or go plunging to the bottom.

There's a children's story called *Hope for the Flowers* that reminds me a little of that game we all seem to play. One bright summer day, a caterpillar called Stripe was aimlessly meandering through a meadow. Suddenly he came across an astonishing sight—a humongous mountain of caterpillars. This caterpillar mountain reached into the clouds and beyond.

These millions of caterpillars were all driven by a common obsession. They all wanted to know what was at the top of this gigantic caterpillar pillar. As Stripe wandered around the base of this squirming mass, he too got caught up in the same overwhelming obsession.

Stripe soon found that moving up the mountain was a struggle. Finally, at tremendous cost to himself and others, Stripe made it to the top of the caterpillar mountain, only to discover . . . *there was nothing there at all!* [1]

How many of us are learning that when we make it to the top of our respective mountains there is really nothing there at all? How many of us are finding that struggling to purchase the newest technological novelty, buy a bigger home, or get that long-awaited promotion doesn't really satisfy us? Deep down I think we all know we are created for more than this.

Steep Slopes and Tough Questions

Let me tell you about a few people I know who are worn out trying to live up to other people's expectations. They are asking questions about what's at the top and what it will cost them to get there.

A dentist in Eugene, Oregon, Allen was working his tail off to create the life and practice expected of an up-and-coming health professional. He continually struggled to enlarge his practice because he believed such growth was synonymous with success. He continued to expand even though he already had more work than he could handle.

He and his wife bought a large, expensive home on a huge estate outside of town because that was expected of professionals like him. Of course, they bought everything on credit to tastefully furnish the home. This debt, combined with mortgage payments, deepened their sense of economic pressure.

When I met Allen, he was spending most of his waking hours either at work or commuting. He could spend little of his meager free time with his wife and two kids because he used it to fix up and maintain their new home and his acreage.

Now you can be sure Allen was respected in the community and at church, though he obviously had little time to be involved with either. He had the prestige and prosperity others only dream of. He was climbing the mountain and by all external indicators doing very well. But he was beginning to question. Was this really a mountain God had asked him to climb?

Or was he simply trying to satisfy other people's expectations?

Janet talked to me after I urged students in her Christian college to put Christ and his mission at the center of their lives. Janet wanted to respond to the challenge but she had a problem with parental pressure. For years she had done everything her parents expected of her. She had gone to the college they picked and majored, as they recommended, in business.

Now she was graduating and felt God was calling her to spend two years on a short-term mission project in the *barrios* of São Paulo, Brazil. So she had gone home at spring break of her senior year to tell her folks. Their response had been immediate and unbending. "We didn't spend sixty thousand dollars sending you to college for that. You get your career established and your IRAs started. Then you can vacation in Brazil if you're still interested." Janet found herself stuck halfway up her parent's mountain, asking herself some tough questions.

As soon as Tom and Sue decided to marry, they found themselves in a peer pressure cooker. They were confronted by a whole new set of expectations from their fellow "baby boomers"—expectations that they move to the affluent suburbs, buy a split-level, and get into serious "nesting."

Tom and Sue had met while working in their church's ministry to Laotian refugees. They wanted to buy a home near the Laotian community. But their peers at church warned, "Property values are terrible in the inner city. The crime rates are high. You'll never make a return on your investment. That's no place to raise kids. We'll help you find a nice house in the suburbs. You can still drive to the city to work with the refugees."

Tom and Sue found themselves stuck at the bottom of somebody else's mountain, trying to separate peer pressure from their sense of Christian calling.

The Mountains of Madison Avenue

It's amazing the number of mountains we are expected to climb in every area of our lives as employees, parents, students, church workers—and, of course, consumers. Listen to the confessions of Erma Bombeck.

> I did as I was told. I was fussy about my peanut butter, fought
> cavities, became depressed over yellow wax buildup. . . . I was
> responsible for my husband's underarms being protected for
> twelve hours. I was responsible for making sure my children
> had a well-balanced breakfast. I alone was carrying the burden
> for my dog's shiny coat. . . . We believed if we converted to all
> the products that marched before our eyes we could be the best,
> the sexiest, the freshest, the cleanest, the thinnest, the smartest
> and the first in our block to be regular. Purchasing for the entire
> family was the most important thing I had to do.[2]

In our upwardly mobile lifestyles, being good consumers is
for many of us the most important thing we do. Shopping has
become a major leisure-time activity. Increasingly our sense of
identity and self-worth is integrally connected to what we buy.
We have come really to believe we are what we own—and that
the more we own, the more we are. Since our entire view of the
better future is seen largely in materialistic terms it isn't difficult
to persuade us to always increase our appetite for new products
and new services.

The folks on Madison Avenue have done a remarkable job
of persuading us to scale their illusory peaks and buy into their
empty dreams. They have tried to convince us that an ever-
increasing level of consumerism is synonymous with happiness. They constantly reveal new needs we didn't know we had,
needs which can only be satisfied by the new products they offer. "Shop till you drop," they urge us; "you deserve it!" Christian and non-Christian alike lockstep up the slippery slopes of
our consumer culture and the shopping mall has replaced the
church as our society's center of "religious" devotion.

Listen to this little jingle for Michelob beer—it sounds like
what caterpillars must have been singing when they began their
scramble up the caterpillar mountain: "You're on your way,
moving up . . . eager to try. You're on your way to the top."
Newsweek predicted that Michelob's light beer promo would become the battle cry of a generation: *"You can have it all."* [3]

CLIMB THAT MOUNTAIN! is our society's persistent refrain.
We are pressured from all sides to scale those peaks because the
good life is waiting for us at the top with the "rich and famous."

But exactly what is waiting for us at the top? Is it indeed the good life? Or something else? Is it worth the sacrifice? Is it worth a little ruthless climbing over our peers? Or have we been sold a bill of goods? Will we find the same thing at the top that Stripe the caterpillar did?

The High Price of High Climbing
—for Participants

Just what is the good life so many North Americans are climbing toward? We tend to see the good life almost exclusively in economic and materialistic terms . . . with a little self-fulfillment tossed in. Cultural anthropologists affirm that for Americans "achievement and success are measured by the quantity of material goods one possesses." [4]

For those who believe that ever-increasing levels of consumption will make us happy, Paul Wachtel has a disquieting word. He reports that, according to social surveys, Americans were much more satisfied with life in 1958 than today—even though we now have many more consumer products.[5]

Not only is there serious question about whether the destination is worth the trip, there is growing evidence that the climb itself isn't doing us much good. Our humanity and spirituality is certainly not enhanced by being stepped on or by climbing over others to make it to the top!

I run into so many Christians who are living lives of hyperstress and chronic burnout. What we are doing to ourselves and our children in this frenetic high-tech society is criminal. We are working so hard to get to the top we are making life along the way unbearable.

Stress has become a national illness whose impact is reflected in troubling mental-health statistics, growing alcohol and drug abuse, breakdown of family life, and escalating suicide rates. Robert Anderson, a physician who has written about stress, says he used to think that 30 to 40 percent of the problems presented by patients were stress-induced. Now he thinks stress may be implicated in 90 percent of ailments.[6]

Even young children are under growing stress to achieve

and get ahead. "The daily schedule of some children, especially those in the suburbs, is fuller than that of a business executive. Children are under pressure to grow up fast socially and excel academically." Drivenness is called the "epidemic of the nineties" and "the applauded addiction" in a recent book.[7]

It's becoming ever clearer that the rat race isn't really the good life. It isn't good for us, for our children, or our environment. We need to say no. We are among the wealthiest, most powerful people in the world. But we are discovering that maintaining and protecting our consumptive lifestyles is one of our major stressors.

Let's bring it right home. How are you doing? What pressures do you live with? What symptoms of stress are you struggling with in your own life? Have you gotten close enough to the top of your mountain to learn whether what's waiting at the top is worth the struggle? Deep down do you suspect there is another mountain, a different dream, a more satisfying way of life? What a tragedy to spend an entire life—like Willy Loman in *Death of a Salesman*—laboring for a false dream. How sad to discover, too late, that "it only looked good from the bottom."

Paul Wachtel's analysis is helpful in enabling us to understand how materialism and economic growth has reached such ascendancy in American society.

> For most of human history people lived in tightly knit communities in which each individual had a specific place and in which there was a strong sense of shared fate. The sense of belonging, of being part of something larger than oneself, was an important source of comfort. In the face of dangers and terrifying mysteries that the lonely individual encountered, this sense of connectedness, along with one's religious faith, which often could hardly be separated from one's membership in the community, was for most people the main way of achieving some sense of security and the courage to go on.[8]

Over the past several centuries, our sense of rootedness and connectedness in Western society has markedly declined. In its place has appeared a kind of isolation in which we as separate individuals and families function more or less autonomously in the larger society. At the center of our lives we find no shared faith or common cause. Instead we attempt to remedy our sense of aloneness, insecurity, and spiritual alienation with consumerism, materialism, and upscaling.

Wachtel insists,

> Our present stress on growth and productivity is, I believe, intimately related to the decline in rootedness. Faced with loneliness and vulnerability that come with deprivation of a securely encompassing community, we have sought to quell the vulnerability through our possessions.[9]

In other words, we are a people possessed by fear. Henri Nouwen shares,

> Fear dominates every part of our being. We think fearfully, we act and react fearfully. Fear has often penetrated our inner selves so deeply that it controls, whether we are aware of it or not, most of our choices and decisions.[10]

In our isolation we live in fear and insecurity. In our materialism we seek to replace the lost intimacy and security of community and faith.

Of course, when we stop to think about it, we *know* our possessions will never satisfy our deepest longings or provide real security. But we *don't* stop to think—at least not long enough to let the reality sink in. We simply put on our clamps, grab pickaxes and ropes, then climb mountains not only to satisfy others but in a futile attempt to pacify our deepest fears and gratify our deepest longings.

The High Price of High Climbing —for Nonparticipants

The North American rat race is not only taking its toll on participants but is also harming the other people with whom we share the planet! By the year 2000, we will share our global habitat with over six billion people. And most statistics indicate that the gap between the planetary rich and the planetary poor is widening dramatically as we approach the twenty-first century.

Well, what does this have to do with our upward mobility? Everything! To the extent that we are caught up in our own lives, our time or money isn't available for ministry to others. At a time when the North American church should be initiating a program of massive mobilization to carry out both the great commission and the great commandment, we are using most of our individual and institutional resources on ourselves.

I believe a major reason so little of our total resources or time are invested in the mission of the church is that we have such heavy demands on our lives. Other peaks and mountains have our attention, resources, and commitment. Even many of our churches have developed upwardly mobile lifestyles.

My hope—indeed, my conviction—is that we can find in Scripture a new sense of purpose for our lives and God's world. We need our sense of Christian responsibility sharpened and our commitment to Christ and his kingdom radically deepened. Above all, I pray we will indeed discover that more significant life to which our God calls us—a new way to live it up that makes a real difference in both our stress-filled lives and God's desperately needy world.

Climbing Another Mountain

Expansive blue skies stretched above Jerusalem as I walked up Mount Zion toward the gates of the Old City. I was traveling in the Middle East on a fact-finding mission and talking to Jews and Arabs, Muslims and Christians, trying to understand the complex problems of that troubled region.

We had the day off. Not having been to Jerusalem, I decided to spend my day as a pilgrim. I visited the Via Dolorosa and could almost hear the crowds calling for our Lord's life. As I entered the church of the Holy Sepulcher, said to be the site of Christ's crucifixion and resurrection, I was moved.

Then as I climbed Mount Zion something surprising happened. It was as though I suddenly found myself surrounded by a vast throng pressing its way up to Jerusalem. Singing.

Dancing. Children on shoulders. Banners streaming. Horns blaring. Outrageous joy. Unspeakable worship. To this day I don't fully understand that experience. But I found myself swept away by the throng and caught up in their song.

Since that remarkable experience I have found a number of others drawn to Jerusalem—that place where God chose to dwell. We do indeed have a better dream and a better mountain to climb. In Isaiah 2 we are told that Mount Zion, the hill of the Lord, will transcend all other mountains.

Isaiah shares many compelling images of God's festive future. Listen to Isaiah 35:1-10.

> The desert and the parched land will be glad;
>   the wilderness will rejoice and blossom.
> Like the crocus, it will burst into bloom;
>   it will rejoice greatly and shout for joy.
> The glory of Lebanon will be given to it,
>   the splendor of Carmel and Sharon;
> they will see the glory of the Lord,
>   the splendor of our God.
> Strengthen the feeble hands,
>   steady the knees that give way;
> say to those with fearful hearts,
>   "Be strong, do not fear;
> your God will come,
>   he will come with vengeance;
> with divine retribution
>   he will come to save you."
> Then will the eyes of the blind be opened
>   and the ears of the deaf unstopped.
> Then will the lame leap like a deer,
>   and the mute tongue shout for joy.
> Water will gush forth in the wilderness
>   and streams in the desert.
> The burning sand will become a pool,
>   the thirsty ground bubbling springs.
> In the haunts where jackals once lay,
>   grass and reeds and papyrus will grow.
> And a highway will be there;
>   it will be called the Way of Holiness.

> The unclean will not journey on it;
>   it will be for those who walk in that Way;
>   wicked fools will not go about on it.
> No lion will be there,
>   nor will any ferocious beast get up on it;
>   they will not be found there.
> But only the redeemed will walk there,
>   and the ransomed of the Lord will return.
> They will enter Zion with singing;
>   everlasting joys will crown their heads.
> Gladness and joy will overtake them,
>   and sorrow and sighing will flee away.
>
> (Isa. 35:1-10, NIV)

It's time for Christians to discover we have a new song of ascents, a new way of life, a new mountain to climb whose majesty overwhelms the piddling peaks of this world. God calls us to life. A life made whole in realization that we are deeply loved. A life made powerful in discovering God uses the foolish to confound the mighty. A life made significant in the incredible realization that God uses broken, ordinary people like you and me to join the Creator God in transforming the world.

The first step we take down our worldly mountains will be the first step up to Jerusalem. Remember the dentist, the student, and the young couple? They are not only asked tough questions regarding the peaks they were struggling to scale; they also took that critically important first step down, which has placed each of them on a new journey up.

The young dentist told me that he had, with difficulty, made it through my book, *The Mustard Seed Conspiracy,* which outlines ways Christians can participate in God's future. And finally Allen and his wife reached a hard decision. They sold their large, expensive estate to buy a more modest home near his work.

Allen was clearly exuberant when I talked to him that second time. He had not only been set free from other people's expectations; he had also been set free to follow his sense of God's dream for his life. He reported that as a consequence of significantly reducing his commuting and the time he invested in maintaining his huge acreage, he had much more time to spend with his family and to invest in ministry to migrant families in Eugene. (By the way, his nine-year-old daughter wasn't as impressed by the decision as the rest of the family. She suggested that they burn the book "before it causes any more trouble.")

Then there was Janet. After talking and praying with leaders in her church, Janet reported that they confirmed God's call on her life for short-term service in Brazil. Janet, deeply respecting her parents, spent a great deal of time trying to help them understand that God's call on her life had to come first.

Subsequently she learned about a new master's of business program at Eastern College designed to train persons to start small businesses among the poor overseas and at home. When she returns from Brazil, Janet hopes to further her business education at Eastern in a way consistent with God's call.

And remember Tom and Susan? As they struggled with the decision of where to live, they realized they were struggling with fears—fears of what other people would think, fears of not living up to other people's expectations. But Henri Nouwen's article about fear helped set them free. Nouwen points out that "fear is one of the most effective weapons in the hands of those who would seek to control us."[11] Yet the first words of the messengers who announced the coming of Christ were, "Don't be afraid." After much thought and discussion, Tom and Susan decided to buy a house in the poorer part of the city, where they could be close to their ministry. As they work, they are learning that "perfect love casts out all fear."

I should say a word about Stripe the caterpillar, too. As the story turns out, Stripe also decided to descend from the top of his mountain. And eventually, through the miracle of metamorphosis, he too found a new way of soaring above the mountains shrinking below him.

The formula is always the same. Our journey up begins with coming down from the pressured peaks of our own and other people's expectations. Then through metamorphosis we, like Stripe, can enjoy a new life of ascents.

As you begin this book, I encourage you to do so with prayer, giving God all your dreams, aspirations, fears, and desires; opening yourself to God's dreams and visions for your life. We can trust our God's love to lead us to a new level of purposeful living within God's new community of ascent.

The Creator God calls us to meaning—to live life fully and significantly. Those who have tasted something of the goodness and purposes of God can never again be satisfied with the "fleshpots of Egypt" or the "splendor of Babylon." We are called to something more.

Because God's love is expressed so compellingly to us in incarnation, we have discovered that we are deeply loved. Because God's grace is communicated so mercifully to us in crucifixion, we are reminded God goes to any cost to give us a new beginning. And because God's call to us is expressed so powerfully in resurrection, we are promised a future made new.

This same God invites us to join with sisters and brothers all over the world to set aside lesser agendas and become part of what God is doing in history to transform a world and redeem a people. The Creator invites us to become a part of a new story.

FOR THOUGHT AND DISCUSSION

1. What specific expectations keep you climbing?
2. What is it costing you in terms of time, relationships, and mental or physical health to scale your peak? What motivates you to keep climbing?
3. Describe the longing within you to find a less stressed, more satisfying way of life . . . that also makes a difference in God's world.

Having trouble keeping it up?

life direction	linkages	consequences
For too many of us life has never been so busy, so stressed, so totally lacking in direction. We feel as though we are carrying the burdens of the world on our backs. And we are having a tough time keeping it up. Never have I run into so many people so exhausted trying to live up to other people's expectations. We don't seem to have any idea how to live it up.	Many of us seem perfectly content to link our lives to other people's expectations and the expectations of the culture and never ask where it is taking us . . . or at what cost.	And of course some of us do reach the summits we are climbing only to discover . . . there is nothing there. Then we are left to count the high human costs of our frantic scrambling, on our own lives and relationships and the larger world we are a part of.

Discerning Half-truths and False Visions

Discerning! From the moment we arrive on Planet Earth, we begin struggling to discern who we are and what we are here for. We are all born into families, churches, and cultures with many different stories and expectations that early shape the direction and character of our lives. Most important, they teach us their notions of what is worth giving our lives to.

Implicit in all our lives are certain images, values, and stories which influence our actions and direct our lives. When we become Christians, we begin the process of sorting out which of these values genuinely belong to the story of God and which we have simply absorbed from the stories around us.

This discerning business isn't easy, and most of us aren't very good at it—we may not even know it is something we need to do! But discernment is essential if we are to be clear about what's up . . . how to find a truly satisfying way of life.

And that's the purpose of this chapter—to enable us to discern more fully the half-truths and full fictions that have be-come a part of our lives. We want to begin to clear the decks so we can more fully embrace God's purposes for our lives and God's world and find a new way up.

But let's be honest. There's nothing tougher than sorting through the false dreams to which we have given our lives. And it's easy to become confused as we do this. Therefore I hope we can be particularly prayerful in this chapter, asking God's Spirit to help us honestly identify dreams, images, and values in our lives that aren't consistent with a biblical vision of God's loving purposes for our lives or our world.

A Step Beyond Confusion

Some people seem to have almost a genetic predisposition toward confusion in this business of finding direction. I have had to come to terms with this tendency in my own life. (Though I have come to think of it as something of a gift. A little well-placed confusion does wonders to keep life from becom-ing boring, predictable, and ordinary.)

Recently, for example, I was traveling from Amsterdam by train to a speaking engagement in a church in Basel, Switzer-land. Such a clear-cut assignment should provide little opportu-nity for confusion—but I managed it!

I confidently climbed on a train marked "Geneva" and ar-rived, after an enjoyable ride, at about two in the afternoon. But as I stepped down from the train, I was surprised to see a friend of mine from Lausanne, Switzerland, running to meet me.

"Hurry! You can still make it," she exclaimed.

"Make what?" I responded.

"The train to Basel. You're not supposed to be in Geneva. You're supposed to be in Basel!"

I stared at her, dumbfounded. She was right. What was I do-ing in Geneva?

As Elaine pushed me on board the train to Basel, she yelled, "You can still make your seven o'clock speaking engagement, so nothing is lost." As the train pulled out of the Geneva station, I waved and called out my thanks—grateful I have learned to wire my travel plans to a friend in each country where I travel. Elaine had received my wire, discerned my confusion, and came to my aid.

Some time later, as the train was pulling out of Zurich, I asked the conductor if we were near Basel. I was determined not to give my proclivity toward chaos any more opportunity to display itself. He replied, "Basel is not far now."

About fifteen minutes later, two Swiss gentlemen sitting across from me got up to get off the train at the next stop. One turned to me and said, "This is your stop. This is where you want to get off."

I quickly shouldered my garment bag and followed them obediently off the train. I found myself in the most modern receiving area I had ever seen—red and blue tile covered the walls, reaching four to five stories above. I looked around for my hosts, whom Elaine had promised to call and inform about my new arrival time. But no one was there to meet me.

For some thirty minutes I tried to call my hosts without success. Finally, I asked at visitor information how much it would cost to take a cab to my destination in Basel. She responded with obvious incredulity, "Well, over a hundred marks."

"Where am I?" I asked.

"At the Zurich International Airport," my informant responded. Sometimes all I need is a little outside help to become even more confused than usual!

I investigated when the next train was headed for Basel. Then I called my hosts, explained the entire fiasco, and told them my train to Basel wouldn't arrive until around nine. I apologized for missing my speaking assignment and thanked them for their hospitality.

As I boarded my third train to Basel, I was more than a little relieved I wouldn't have to speak. I hadn't had an opportunity to sleep in almost twenty-four hours. I hadn't had a shower for three days. I needed a shave, my hair was a mess, and I wasn't prepared to speak because I didn't know who my audience was.

When I finally arrived in Basel a little after nine, every cell in my body was looking forward to a hot shower and a clean bed. There were my hosts. I began bubbling with apologies, but Johann exclaimed, "Not to worry. We sent the congregation out for coffee and told them to be back by a quarter after nine."

I stood dazed. There wasn't even time to shave, comb my hair, or write down a little outline. On the way to the church I found my Bible, selected a verse, and prayed.

But I've discovered that once you're on a roll nothing can stop you. I shouldn't have worried about my message. The young woman they asked to translate for me had never done it before. I am convinced that very gracious congregation had no idea what I was trying to say. And I must have been a rumpled, bedraggled delight to look at.

Even if you don't have my predisposition toward confusion, it seems an inevitable part of the human condition. And there is no area in which confusion plays greater havoc than in the ways we seek to direct our lives. Remarkably, many of us are unaware of our confusion because we haven't even noticed the alien stories to which we have given ourselves. We simply seem to dance to someone else's tune and never question the melody.

If we want to move beyond confusion and embrace more fully the story of God, we must first identify the stories we are living for. And we particularly need to examine the visions of the better future that are a part of these stories to see how they compare with God's vision.

Some False Visions of the Better Future

We live in a world filled with thousands of stories that promise a wide variety of visions for the good life and a better future. They reflect very different value systems and take us to very different destinations.

For example when I was in Nepal, a young Muslim driving a truck in front of us inadvertently struck and killed a cow. The missionary sitting next to me said, "It would have been better for that young man to have run over a person instead of killing a cow—because killing a cow will put him in jail for life!"

What vision of the future in a Hindu society would sentence a young man to life imprisonment for killing a cow? Incarnation. Hindus believe we are recycling through time and space. And they believe that the sacred cow is one of the highest forms in the cycles of reincarnation. The Hindu legal system reflects that view of the future.

Shirley MacLaine and other New Age spokespersons offer a pop version of reincarnation for those who seem chronically to mess up their lives. Not to worry, in one of your next lives you can get it right, they suggest.

With the collapse of the Soviet Union, Marxism as an ideology is in decline all over the world. However, there are still those true believers who envision the better future as a centrally planned, egalitarian workers' state.

Most Americans are not attracted to a Marxist vision of the better future, Hinduism, or even a pop "New Age" view. We are seduced by another vision, rooted in the Enlightenment, which permeates all of Western society, including the church—buying into the Western dream and all the values that go with it.

To help us examine familiar stories closer to the lives of most Western Christians, I want to introduce four hypothetical couples. They are typical of people I meet in my travels. Let me emphasize that these couples are not representative of all mainliners, evangelicals, or rightwingers. They simply represent some folks from such groups. And they are overstated a bit to make the point.

As a consequence, these examples will probably not fully connect with our own visions and values. I hope, however, that they will help us discern some areas where our stories and values may differ from the biblical story without our even realizing it. At the least, I hope these examples provoke questions.

In each story we will ask "what seems to be the image of the better future to which the couple are giving their lives?" Then we will examine whether the better future they are working for will really enable them to create a way of life they can love. . . . A way of life consistent with the purposes of God.

Couple # 1: Brent and Becky Hightower—"Traveling to the Land of Evermore"

Brent Hightower and Becky Williams met during a pizza eating contest on an InterVarsity spring outing at Malibu. Becky beat all comers. Brent was impressed both by her remarkable capacity and winning smile.

He struck up a conversation. They discovered they were both sophomore business majors at Claremont College and had been raised Presbyterian. During spring quarter, Becky and Brent began studying together. Their relationship got pretty rocky during their junior year. But as they began their senior year they decided to go for it.

They planned to marry immediately after graduation, while their parents and friends were still in town. Becky's parents financed an elaborate wedding. And Brent's parents sprang for the cost of a honeymoon in Hawaii.

While prowling the back streets of Lahaina and lounging on the beaches of Maui, Becky and Brent began talking about their future. Brent wanted to get a position on international finance; Becky's chosen field was quality management.

After returning from their honeymoon, they moved all of Becky's possessions into Brent's small studio apartment in Pasadena and began looking for jobs. They applied for a range of openings in southern California. But they were dismayed to learn that without experience or MBAs, they had little hope of starting out in their chosen fields. Running low on resources, they decided to take any kind of job they could get in a good organization, then work to move up.

Late one Saturday evening, Brent's dad called to tell of an opening for a delivery van driver for Microsoft in Seattle. Brent got the position. Two weeks later he and Becky were driving her old Honda north to Seattle, pulling a small trailer with all their earthly belongings. On their arrival, Becky found an entry-level position as a teller.

They were both glad to have jobs and some money coming in. But they were frustrated. They had settled for low-paying jobs they could have had right out of high school.

However, they began their life together with the same energy and optimism they had invested in their studies at Claremont. Brent's parents helped them with a down payment on a one bedroom condo in Bellevue. They used plastic to furnish their new home with stylish contemporary furniture plus a $1,700 entertainment center.

Needing two cars to drive to their respective jobs, they put the remainder of their savings down on a new maroon Audi. Brent and Becky felt they owed themselves a little treat after four years of struggle at Claremont. So they also bought a small sailboat on credit. Sailing had been an integral part of their childhood family lives.

For the first three months the Hightowers were riding high. In July they focused on settling in and decorating their new condo. In August they spent most of their free time sailing in the San Juan Islands and camping. September was packed with entertaining new friends, checking out some of Seattle's nicer restaurants, and even attending the Young Marrieds class at University Presbyterian Church a couple of times.

The Hightowers were thoroughly enjoying the Northwest, their new friends, and their life together. They were pretty sure that they knew how to live it up.

However, as the cool breezes of autumn blew across Puget Sound, Brent and Becky experienced a chilling come-down. They found themselves buried in an avalanche of bills they had been putting off. They were getting an increasing number of threatening notices from creditors. Then their sailboat was re-possessed. Most embarrassing of all, their gas was turned off for nonpayment. Nothing like this had ever happened before to them or their families of origin.

Plastic would no longer bail them out. They didn't want their parents to know about their plight. They sat there in their chilly kitchen poring over their finances, trying to figure out why the bottom had fallen out of their lives.

The first discovery they made was that it really wasn't possible on their incomes to enjoy the lifestyles with which they had been raised. Second, they began seriously to question whether the lifestyle aspirations with which they had been raised were really the good life. They were no longer sure of what was up or how to get there. They began taking a good hard look at what they wanted for the future.

What Is the Better Future?

To understand where the Hightowers and many of the rest of us get off the track, we need to ask this: What are the aspirations and stories to which we have given our lives? Where did those stories come from?

Essentially the storytellers of the Enlightenment told us a new story. They assured us that if we cooperated with natural law, all of Western society would progress economically and technologically. The Western dream promises that if we cooperate with the natural order we will enjoy lives of ever-increasing influence. We will be transported, by the magic marketplace, to the Land of Evermore. The North American dream, therefore, sees the better future in terms of ever-increasing materialism, individualism, and consumerism.

Someone has written that "Marxism says all there is is matter. Capitalism says all that matters is matter." But they are both inherently materialistic visions of the better future, both born of the Enlightenment, both lacking any larger sense of transcendence.

How in the world have people of faith been seduced by such a dream? I suspect where it innocently begins is that we all want what's best for our kids. Of course, there is nothing wrong with that. But because of the pervasive, insidious influence of the North American dream we define what's "best" in largely economic and materialistic terms.

Look at the hidden "curriculum" of our homes and families. Many parents surround their kids with a surplus of consumer goods, including their own private stereos, TVs, VCRs, phones, Walkmans, and eventually cars. The clear message in Christian and non-Christian homes alike is that such possessions are what make the good life. Every Christmas looks like the department store blew up in the living room!

I am sure Brent and Becky's notion of how to live it up came largely from the upper-middle class Christian homes they were raised in. Until they hit the wall financially, they had never given much thought to the stories, dreams, and aspirations to which they had rather thoughtlessly given their lives. They never questioned the destination . . . the Land of Evermore.

I doubt that their parents ever questioned what the good life was, either, or where they were most likely to find it. The popular wisdom then and now is that the very best place to raise kids is in the affluent suburbs.

I believe, however, that the affluent suburbs are probably the hardest place to raise kids with Christian values. Although the insidious influence of the North American dream pervades all society, it is particularly relentless in suburbs . . . where the young are expected to dress alike, hit the slopes on the same weekend, and subscribe to the same status-driven values.

Recently I addressed a Mennonite PTA meeting in an upper-middle class suburban community near Pittsburgh, Pennsylvania. I raised questions in passing about the status driven values promoted in the suburbs. A parent came up to me afterward, obviously miffed, and challenged my critique.

Then she shifted gears and declared, "My daughter, who is a junior at the Mennonite high school in our suburban community, is so angry at her father and me she hasn't spoken to us for three weeks!"

"Why is she angry?" I asked.

"Because she has to be seen being driven to school in a car over three years old," she said.

I responded, "That's what I was saying about the suburbs. You didn't buy a house . . . you bought an entire set of status-driven values that are an integral part of living in many affluent suburban communities."

I continued, "If you had raised your daughter in Pittsburgh she would have been glad to have a ride to school in any car!"

The first generations of Mennonites in the U.S. and Canada generally lived on the farm. A number of subsequent generations moved to the cities to do urban ministry. The present generation, like virtually all the Christian young, are headed for the suburbs. I seriously doubt the unique Anabaptist witness of the Mennonite community will survive one generation of affluent suburban living.

Wherever we live or raise our young in North America, the culture is conditioning them to become more self-involved, more committed to making a buck instead of making a life.

Listen to this troubling analysis by Robert Cole, a leading psychologist who specializes in studying the North American young.

> Very little is asked of a lot of American children with regard to compassion and thinking of others. The emphasis is to cultivate the individuality and self-importance of a child. One sees home after home where children are encouraged to look out for themselves and get what they can. Very little emphasis is put on pointing the child's eyes and ears away from himself or herself and towards others.[1]

For over twenty years, Alexander Austin has studied college freshmen nationwide, and his research confirms Cole's indictment. Twenty years ago, the dominant reason for going to college among college freshmen was "finding a meaningful philosophy of life." Today that value has slipped to number eight on the list. And predictably, "Being well off financially" has soared to the top of the list for 70 percent of all freshmen.[2]

Not only is the Dream—reinforced through Christian homes, schools, and churches—corrupting the aspirations and values of the Christian young. The efforts of the young, like the Hightowers, to fully realize that dream seriously threatens the future of the church as well.

As I point out in *Wild Hope*, the North American young are entering the economy at a different time than their parents or grandparents. As a consequence, everything middle class, from housing to health care, is ten to twenty times more expensive than thirty years ago. But the income of those under thirty has not kept pace.

That means that while their parents and grandparents were typically able to buy the house on a single income, young people today have to have two and increasingly three incomes. Some will never be able to buy the single family detached home. And growing numbers of the young, following the upscale models of their parents' lifestyles, are belatedly discovering they can't make ends meet. Many are moving back home with their parents, becoming the "hidden homeless."

The upshot of all of this is that the under-thirties are going to have significantly less discretionary time and money than their parents and grandparents. World Vision reports that those under thirty are already giving fully 50 percent less than those over thirty. Therefore, as over the next three decades the under-thirties move into leadership in our churches, they won't be able to support the church in the style to which the church is accustomed. As a consequence, I believe the mission capability of the entire Western church is in serious peril as we enter a new century. All because we sold the Christian young the wrong dream . . . the American dream with a little Jesus overlay.

The first step up is to come down from the false stories and fraudulent aspirations to which we have given our lives and to face this reality: if the church is to have a future, we must all find a biblical alternative to the essentially self-seeking materialistic values of the Western dream. We must find a new destination to replace the Land of Evermore. . . . A new way up.

Let's look at three other couples who have given themselves to various versions of the Western dream but somewhat different notions of the better future.

Couple #2: Ernest and Fran Liberman—Doing What's Best for Myself *First*

Ernie and Fran also met in college twenty-plus years ago, while working on the first Earth Day project. Earth Day 1970 was an important milestone in the environmental movement which helped the young get caught up in the activism of that era.

Now the Libermans are forty-somethings and settled. One night over dinner they were reflecting on those days of activism and change. As they were describing some of the protests they were involved in to their teenagers, Jeremy and Jennifer, Jeremy quietly pushed a piece of veal scallopini around the perimeter of his plate.

Not receiving any feedback at all, Ernie plied them for a response. "Come on, I know you're both involved in green groups at school."

Jennifer suddenly looked up from her plate and responded, "What happened?"

"What do you mean what happened?" Fran replied.

"Look, you guys aren't even marginal . . . you don't recycle, you don't compost, you drive two cars that get terrible gas mileage. And you're still buying this factory-raised veal! What happened? How did you get so far away from this activism stuff?"

Before Fran and Ernie could gather their wits, Jeremy blurted, "Out of here! Play practice in fifteen." The Libermans sat there alone, staring at a plate of cold veal.

Finally Ernie asked, "What happened? Have we really changed that much?"

Fran said, "I don't want to get into it!"

But Ernie, shaken, insisted; they began tracing back twenty years of their life together.

"Remember after we graduated from the University of Chicago in 1974, we stayed on so I could get my master's degree in political science," Ernie reflected. "The whole reason for hanging in there was so I could continue to work in political activism somewhere."

"But then I got accepted into the master's program in social work at Columbia University and we moved and the only job you could find was research at IBM. And before I finished my comps, motherhood overtook me . . . and Jeremy arrived two months after graduation," Fran said.

"You're right, Fran, everything began to change way back there. I got fed up with the politics of "Big Blue" but instead of trying to get back into some kind of social activism, I settled for another good paying research position in electronics and we moved here to Beacon, New York."

Ernie continued, "I *am* a little put out at our two 'politically correct' offspring. They wouldn't be attending the private schools with a green curriculum or be able to go on study tours to Europe in the summer if I hadn't worked my buns off for the 'establishment' and you hadn't taken a position in industrial relations."

Fran added, "Jennifer and Jeremy may not be aware of the church committees on social justice and the environment we've served on."

She continued, "But I don't think we realize how much we

have changed, Ernie . . . and maybe it's time to deal with that. I think I traded my involvement in activism and feminism for a comfortable home, a good career, and yoga and T.M. classes. You cashed in your activism for a good job and these long weekends away to focus on New Age channeling and sorting out your Inner Life."

"Fran, I know you don't appreciate what these weekends do for me but—"

"Look, Ernie, whatever you're into is cool . . . but between the long hours at work and these weekends away, we sure haven't had much of a relationship for the past three years."

"Hey, I thought we were in this together, Fran."

"For years I thought so too, Ernie, but too much has changed! I want to start life over again. It's nothing against you. I've been going to a therapist for about a year and didn't tell you. She has encouraged me to pay serious attention to my own needs and feelings and agrees with me that I need to do what's best for myself first. This isn't the way I wanted to tell you . . . but it's over, Ernie."

It was after midnight and Ernie was still sitting alone in the dark, stunned. He kept asking himself over and over, *"How could things have changed so much and I was so oblivious?"* In a few brief hours, the Libermans' world had turned upside-down. And neither Ernie and Fran seemed to have any idea what was up.

What Is the Better Future?

Until Jennifer's probing questions, it would have appeared to an outside observer that the Libermans had a pretty clear notion of what the good life was. In spite of their youthful social activism, the Libermans had been raised like the Hightowers to believe the good life consisted of getting a piece of the great American Dream. But there were some important differences.

For one, the Libermans hit the economy at a much better time than the Hightowers. They were thus more successful than Brent and Becky in reaching the Land of Evermore. But it was clear that both Fran and Ernie had made compromises to secure their comfortable lifestyles. And they were both struggling with the obvious contradictions.

It should be pointed out, however, that they didn't want the Western dream just for themselves. Like most liberals, they wanted the poor to get a little taste of the dream, too . . . as long as the cost wasn't too great. For them, being Congregationalists and liberal Democrats was part of the same parcel. Neither group questioned the inherent legitimacy of the Western dream, nor did the Libermans. They believed they could enable the poor to board the escalator to the Land of Evermore simply by supporting liberal legislation and social policies.

This commiment to the liberal agenda runs so deep for the Libermans that they, like many in their church, have almost a congenital need to be front edge advocates of whatever is socially progressive at the moment . . . often with little regard for biblical mandate.

But perhaps what distinguishes the Libermans and many other "baby boomers" from those who are both younger and older is that their view of the good life is not limited to the essentially economic aspirations of the Dream. They want a piece of the rock and self-actualization, too. Typically they want a spirituality that demands little of them and others self-fulfillment that affords them the greatest level of personal freedom.

In his important work, *Habits of the Heart*, Robert Bellah describes the essentially economic aspirations of the consumer culture as "utilitarian individualism." Bellah calls the recent preoccupation with self-actualization "expressive individualism."[3]

Daniel Yankelovich in his classic, "New Rules," argues convincingly that the "baby boomer" generation values personal fulfillment even more than economic accumulation. This change of values has fundamentally altered the way many of us approach life.

Yankelovich states,

The ethics of self-fulfillment discards many of the traditional rules of personal conduct. They permit more secular freedom, for example, and they put less emphasis on sacrifice "for its own sake." . . . in place of the old self-denial ethic, we find people who refuse to deny themselves anything not out of a bottomless appetite, but on the strange new moral principle "I have a duty to myself."[4]

It was through this "strange, new moral principle" that Fran justified her shattering announcement. And through that same principle millions have justified the breakup of families and sometimes the abandonment of children.

While the singularly materialistic aspirations of the Western dream compromise our spirituality, undermine our humanity, and imperil God's creation, this new obsessive preoccupation with personal freedom threatens the very fabric of human society. This radical autonomy (also born of the Enlightenment) places at serious risk the future of family, community, and church. Tragically, Ernie discovered this isn't the way up.

Then there are some who, working from a more conservative faith, have a different notion of what the better future looks like. This view, to which we now turn, unwittingly fosters a divided and contradictory view of the future.

Couple #3: Rich and Piety Duellway—"Waiting for Soul Rescue and Working for Fat City"

Rich's exhaustion was evident as he struggled to blow out the thirty-five candles on the large German chocolate cake. He had been working nearly seventy hours a week at a rug cleaning business he owned and also oversaw the finances of his church—The New Life Center.

The four thousand member congregation had just completed construction of a huge new facility and parking lot on seventy acres in Tigard, Oregon. Rich found himself on the phone day and night talking with contractors, church elders, and members of the pastoral staff.

He and his wife, Piety, had become Christians ten years earlier and had been a part of the New Life Center since its beginning.

As Piety cut the cake, she said, "I bet you can't guess what I would have wished for, honey, if I had blown out those candles." Before Rich could respond she said "A big new house!"

"Dear, we have a lovely three bedroom, two-bath home with this large family room. With two kids, don't you really think this is all we need?"

The two twelve-year-old twins, Mark and Sara, began fighting over the biggest piece of cake while Piety, smiling, changed the subject.

Mark and Sara are an energetic pair. Mark has just discovered the opposite "species," and Sara spends most of her free time with her girlfriends shopping. They both spend most weekends with the junior highs at church.

The Duellways had wanted Piety not to work so she could be there when the kids got home from school. But her shopping obsession made it impossible for them to make it on Rich's income, even though he had increased his work load 20 percent in the last year. Piety was one of those people who rarely ran into a bargain she didn't love.

The Duellways worked out a compromise. Piety took a part-time secretarial position at Tigard Christian Academy where their twins attended. That way she could be in touch with them during the school day. And it helped them not only to pay a few more bills but also to keep paying their double pledge to their church's building program.

They were just getting used to their two-career schedule when the New Life senior pastor called. He asked them to spend a week of their vacation attending the National Charismatic Conference in Kansas City. Sara and Mark immediately put up a storm of protest because they realized it would mean postponing Disneyland for the third straight year. But their efforts were futile. Their parents had an unqualified loyalty to their church and immediately began planning for the trip.

In a few months the entire family and seven large suitcases were flying the "friendly skies" to Kansas City. After checking in at the Hilton, they went to the first plenary session.

As Rich, Piety, and the twins entered the huge main auditorium, they saw a large banner stretched across the stage which read "Even So Come Quickly." They joined in singing, "This world is not my home, I am just passing through," as they found seats near the back.

No sooner had the singing stopped than a large man with a booming voice stood and offered a spontaneous prophetic word. "In these last days," he said, "as the world worsens, do not give up hope. If you persevere, you will be rescued for eternal life in the clouds before the final destruction."

Rich and Piety stood with hands raised and eyes shut, thanking God, while their kids wrestled over a video game. Piety had come wanting a personal word from the Lord for her life. While she agreed with the prophetic word just shared, it wasn't what she needed.

After lunch, the family divided up. Rich went to a leadership meeting for the men. Piety went to a women's prayer and praise meeting. The twins went to the tryout for the youth chorus.

As Piety entered the women's meeting, a tall woman with a large inflated blond hairdo and a frilly red dress was welcoming the attendees.

After some 500 women crowded into the lounge, the tall blond prayed, then began to speak. "Ladies, God loves you . . . and he wants you to have the very best in every area of your life and family. Don't you dare settle for less!" She interrupted herself, "I believe God is giving me a special word for someone here today . . . listen to God's word for your life! The Lord wants you to prove him faithful. Give him an opportunity to bless your life with prosperity and success. Trust God for that beautiful new home and all the lovely things you have ever dreamed of to fill it."

Piety had both hands up in the air. She praised God as tears ran down her face. As soon as the session was over, she bolted from the room, saw Rich in the foyer, and ran up to him, almost knocking over a sofa.

"Honey, what's up?" he asked. "I just got confirmation" she exclaimed, "that we're supposed to buy that beautiful Grand Marqui house I saw in the Key Biscayne development! Not only that, we're to trust God for all of the furnishings to go with it!"

Rich mentally added the price tag. The house Piety was talking about was an oversized 3,600 square foot split-level with a price tag of over $700,000. The furnishings she wanted might cost another $100,000.

Before he could estimate the cost of landscaping the lot, Piety had grabbed his hand. She squeezed it tightly as she energetically prayed, "Thank you for your faithfulness in meeting all our needs and blessing our lives. Amen!"

Instead of praying, Rich stared at the floor, wondering how in the world they would pay for this new "step of faith." Under his breath he murmured, "Even so, come quickly."

Images of a Better Future

The Duellways not only share with the other two couples an unqualified commitment to the aspirations of the Dream, they have added a whole new dimension. Their church teaches that their ability continually to expand their consumer appetites is evidence of their growing spirituality and faith. But as you can sense, Rich is beginning to question whether he has enough faith and income to pay for the gigantic new home "God wants to bless his family with."

What sets this couple apart from the others even more than their "spirit-led" consumerism is their divided view of the future. On the one hand, the Duellways and many other conservative Protestants hold an optimistic view of North America's economic future. They believe the economy will continue to grow and that it's God's job to guarantee them a generous piece of that growth.

The Duellways, like many conservative Christians, are caught up in what I call the "Evangelical Distortion." They see God as a coconspirator with their agendas who helps them get what they want out of life—bigger homes, better paying jobs, parking places when they go downtown. God is seen as a cosmic bellhop in the sky obligated to transport Christians like the Duellways to a very affluent version of the Land of Evermore.

On the other hand, the Duellways and many of their conservative Protestant counterparts hold a pessimistic view of the world's future. Their endtimes teachings have persuaded them that while the economy is getting better, the world as a whole is just as inevitably getting worse. (The apparent contradiction of these two distinct views of the future seems to elude many evangelical and charismatic believers.)

Most conservative Protestants I work with unquestioningly embrace such a fatalistic view of the future and a degenerative view of history. They don't believe that even the Creator God can bring about any major social changes this side of the second coming. They constantly misquote Christ's words, "the poor we have with us always," as justification for their non-involvement and as confirmation of their conviction that everything *has* to get worse.

I doubt that most of these good people prayed the Berlin Wall would come down or the Soviet Union would collapse, because they believe nothing at the national or international level can truly get better. "In these last days" we can get a few more people in the lifeboat, of course—but no real societal change can take place before Christ returns.

Their hope is that before everything inevitably moves into the final period of destruction, their disembodied souls will be rescued for a nonmaterial existence in the clouds. These folks really believe that "this world is not our home" and God's good creation has no part in God's final redemption.

Recently while speaking at a leading Christian college, I asked the students, "What imagery comes to mind when you think of the future of God?"

They responded, "Heaven."

"What imagery comes to mind when you think of heaven?"

They replied, "Clouds, harps, and angels' wings."

Many conservative Protestants worry that New Agers will undermine their faith. They fail to recognize that the Greeks dittled our minds centuries ago. It was the Greeks, not the He-brews, who taught that the material world is inherently evil and we need to escape from it to a non-material spiritual existence.

Lesslie Newbigin declares that looking forward to such a disembodied existence in the clouds isn't biblical. "For the bib-

lical writer, continued existence as a disembodied soul is something not to be desired, but feared with loathing." [5] When the
Bible speaks of salvation, it teaches our resurrection as whole
persons—mind, body, soul, and spirit—who will be part of a
new heaven and earth (as we will discuss in the next chapter).

I believe the powers of darkness are working through end-
time fantasies to persuade one of the best-educated and most
affluent groups of Christians in the history of the world to believe that they can't really make a difference. All these good
people are told by Christian leaders that all they can hope for is
getting a piece of Fat City now (while the getting is still good)
and wait for soul rescue in the clouds by-and-by.

To illustrate the insanity of this view of the future, let me
share one example. Reportedly one leading author of prophecy
books has invested the profits from these books predicting the
imminent end of the world in *long-term* American growth
bonds.

Now clinging to such contradictory views of the future at the
same time should tear people apart. But Christians like the
Duellways seem oblivious to the contradictions. They are content to work for Fat City now and wait for soul rescue by-and-
by.

Couple #4: Frank and Liberty Amright—"Erecting a Super State for Jesus"

It was after 11:00 p.m. when Frank drove his old pickup
truck into the garage on a warm Arizona night. Liberty could
tell as soon as he stepped into their large trailer home that
something was the matter.

She waited quietly as he rubbed his big hands together.
"They showed a video tonight at the Christian Confederation
meeting; it's worse than we thought. Since the Democrats took
over in Washington, the humanists have stepped up their efforts to destroy the family, undermine the church, and take
away our guns." He took a sip of coffee and added, "The speaker said we have maybe five years before they finish their takeover of all American institutions."

"Frank, you said that the Christian Confederation had not only gained control of the local Republican precinct here in Scottsdale but precincts across the country. Won't that be enough to turn the tide and take America back?"

"I don't know, Liberty. We don't have much time. Satan has launched an all-out assault to destroy God's chosen nation and to set the stage for the establishment of a one-world humanist government and the reign of the antichrist. We're going to have to invest more time and money supporting the Confederation and pray it's enough."

Just then, the phone rang. "It's for you, Frank. It sounds like Bud Sharpnik, and he's upset."

Frank got up slowly and eased over to the phone. "Hi, Bud. Didn't expect to talk to you again tonight. What's kicking? Firetrucks where? Bud, I'll see you in thirty-five minutes!"

Frank rushed to the door. "Somehow the Christian Confederations office building caught fire. Don't wait up for me."

As Frank drove up, the Confederation's building was engulfed in flames. The firemen were trying to preserve the two buildings on either side. Bud shook his hand.

Frank said, "It doesn't look like there's much to do. Did we get our files, computers, or anything out?"

"Not a shred," Bud replied. "It's really suspicious how fast it went up. Chief says it's too early to tell how it began. But there's no way we'll ever replace the names we collected. We had the Confederation membership files for the entire Southwest."

Frank shuffled his old cowboy boot in the brown lawn and turned his back on the fire. "Bud, can you and the other elders meet me for lunch tomorrow at Bertha's place to figure out what the Confederation should do next?"

"No problem."

Feedcaps lined the counter at Bertha's as Frank entered and joined the Confederation's inner circle over coffee and lunch.

Keith Ewing came in the door right behind him. "Hey Frank, you got a minute? Heard about the fire. I am working on an article about the fire and the Confederation for the *Scottsdale Daily*."

Frank turned uneasily in his chair. "Morning, Keith, we're kinda busy right now."

"One quick question—did the Confederation lose its files?"

"Keith, we'll have a statement for the press on Monday— we'll talk to you then."

Frank turned back to the table. "Someone told me that that young reporter is a member of the A.C.L.U. I have no interest in giving our opponents more information than we need to."

Bud chirped in, "It's interesting that Ewing is so curious about what we lost in the fire. I called the national office. They're flying out a troubleshooter to help us investigate and continue our momentum. We *will* gain control of all precincts of the Republican Party in this part of God's country!"

Frank had grown up in an all-white neighborhood in Atlanta, in a blue collar home. As a teenager, he was turned off by the social changes taking place in Atlanta and joined the John Birch Society. After a tour of duty in the Marines, he went home, married Liberty, and got his truck repair business established. They started attending a local Baptist church. It was during that time that he read Tim LaHaye's *Battle for the Mind*. Frank embraced LaHaye's belief that America was being undermined by a conspiracy of secular humanists.

Not surprisingly, in the 1980s Frank and Liberty got involved with the Moral Majority, the National Rifle Association, and the Religious Roundtable. In the 1990s they felt they could no longer contend with growing liberal influences in Atlanta. So they moved to a rural area outside of Scottsdale. But even in Arizona they decided to home school their kids to avoid exposing them to the humanist influences in the public schools.

As soon as Frank heard about Christian Confederation, he joined. He liked the Confederation goal of controlling the Republican Party and through the Party taking back America for God. The Confederation aim of restoring traditional American values was one he cared about passionately. He had only been involved for six months and he was moved into leadership and went back to Virginia Beach for training.

Now the Amrights find themselves in the center of a grass roots right wing movement that is slowly changing the character of the Republican Party. Frank and Liberty couldn't be happier about the cause to which they have given their lives.

Bud came by the Amright's place with John Barnes, a national coordinator from the Christian Confederation. "Frank, we have some important information," Bud greeted him at the door. "Our national leadership is concerned about this fire. We hired an exceptional detective from Phoenix, a former FBI agent. Here's the report. Witnesses saw two cars with out-of-state plates parked down the street after you guys left the meeting. We got lucky—a local cop wrote down one of the plates and we ran it. A real hard case from Berkeley that has been identified with virtually every liberal organization from the free speech days, only—" Barnes was interrupted by the phone.

"Frank here."

"Frank, this is the Scottsdale fire chief, Sam Johnson. I know you must be anxious to learn what we found. Apparently someone left the coffee pot on after you guys left your meeting. Our investigation indicates that the fire began with a defective cord on the coffee pot. I'll be sending a letter confirming our findings for your insurance company. I hope this puts your mind at ease. Hello. . . . Mr. Amright . . . are you still there?"

What Is the Better Future?

The Amrights not only want what the other three couples want, a piece of the Dream, they believe it is their God-given destiny. However, unlike the other couples, Frank and Liberty have committed themselves to a vision that calls them beyond themselves. They're aiming to erect a superstate for Jesus. Like many on the religious right, they really believe if they take back America they can avert the dreaded one-world government takeover and see God's reign established.

To understand the religious right you need to understand not so much what they think or believe but rather what they are afraid of. They live in absolute terror of a humanist conspiracy that will set the stage for the establishment of a godless one world government. Francis Schaeffer gave us the term "secular humanism" and Tim LaHaye gave us the conspiratorial definition. LaHaye explains what has gone wrong with America in his bestselling book, *Battle for the Mind*. Without offering a shred of proof, he alleges that a group of aging humanists who have signed something called the "Humanist Manifesto" have already taken over America.

He insists that this small band of humanists has taken over all public schools, all state colleges and universities, all major newspapers, television and radio stations and, of course, all labor unions and liberal organizations. LaHaye alleges that these Humanists are conspiring through this network to take over America and create the one-world, antichrist regime.

In this book I am arguing that we are not only in danger of a conspiratorial take over but we have misdefined the secularism that threaten us. Popularly understood "secular humanists" are those people who are for abortion, gay rights and a liberal political agenda. Conservative Christians not finding themselves anywhere on that list mistakenly assume that we are pure as the driven snow. Nothing could be further from the truth. It is time for us to come down off our self-righteous arrogance and wake up to the fact that we are being eaten alive by a secularism we have totally failed to recognize . . . a secularism that is as present in conservative churches as it is in secular culture. One of the primary purposes of this book is to offer an alternative view of "secular humanism" with all of its imaged enemies without . . . failing to recognize the malignant cancer of materialism, individualism and self-seeking within the church.

With the unexpected collapse of the "Evil Empire," the religious right lost not only its cosmic enemy but the agent it believed Satan would use to institute a one-world society. Now these rightwingers are floundering, seeking new enemies worthy of their wrath. In addition to secular humanists, their list includes environmentalists, feminists, and politic liberals.

To counter the terror of this one-world takeover, the religious right has created a new messianic nationalism that bears little resemblance to historic Christian faith. Rightwingers have rewritten the biblical doctrines of Creation, Fall, redemption. Their revisionist story of creation begins with a second creation—the creation of America. In their revisionist view of redemption, God has chosen the U.S. to replace the transna-

tional Church of Jesus Christ as the agent of God's purposes.
Gabriel Fackre points out that

> perhaps the greatest departure from Christian doctrine by the
> religious right is its transfer of the special covenant from the
> elect of God in the particular history of the children of Israel to
> anot'.er people. The functional elevation of America to the place
> of a chosen nation adds to the Christian story a chapter which is
> not in the Book.[6]

Fackre is right. There is no biblical basis for this brand of
messianic nationalism. Now if this kind of civil religion doesn't
come from Scripture, where does it come from? It emerges, I
believe, from a particularly "creative" reading of history which
argues that America is a unique creation of God, raised high
above all other nations.

Listen to Jerry Falwell, a leader of the religious right: "I believe America has reached the pinnacle of greatness unlike any
other nation because our founding fathers established laws on
the principles recorded in the laws of God." [7]

But three leading evangelical historians, Mark Noll, Nathan
Hatch, and George Marsden can't find any basis in their reading
of American history to substantiate this self-serving nationalistic view. In fact, in their important book, *In Search of Christian
America,* they argue that any objective reading of American history leads to a very different conclusion. They assert,

> We feel a careful study of the facts of history shows that early
> America does not deserve to be considered uniquely, distinctly,
> or even predominantly Christian, if we mean by the word
> "Christian" a state of society reflecting the ideas presented in the
> Scripture.[8]

Of course I believe God was involved in the founding of our
nation . . . as in every nation. But though the nation's founders
made reference to Scripture, I believe the U.S. political order is
more profoundly based on principles coming from the Enlightenment. In their efforts to provide a basis for their ideology, the
religious right have rewritten U.S. history.

Robert Webber accurately points out that messianic nationalism "both baptizes Americanism and politicizes the church." [9] What actually happens is that the church becomes subservient to the nationalistic ideology of the religious right.

This radically alters the definition of Christian mission. Instead of defining Christian mission as our efforts to extend God's love by word and deed to the escalating human needs that fill our world, leaders of the right have politicized Christian mission. They would have us believe that our new mission is to take power politically in order to take America back. Some, like the reconstructionists, not only want to take power, they want to do away with democracy. They aim to create a theocratic state in which the "men of God" rule. This is an unwelcome Christian version of Islamic extremism.

In the 1970s and 1980s, the religious right tried to win political power and influence by gaining favor with the Republican White House. Now leaders of the right have changed their strategy and are trying to secure power at the grass roots level—in Republican precincts and local elections. To the extent this "stealth movement" is successful, it is likely to fragment the Republican party and polarize U.S. society.

Quite honestly most evangelical and charismatic Christians I have talked with in Britain, Australia and New Zealand are appalled at the way in which their conservative counterparts in the United States chronically confuse the agendas of our country with the agendas of the kingdom. They simply can't understand how we confuse flag and cross and insist faith in Christ somehow obligates us to be conservative republicans.

Understandably, many good-hearted believers like the Amrights are concerned about changes in U.S. society that affect everything from family life to moral issues. Leaders of the political right have skillfully used these legitimate concerns to draw many evangelicals, Mennonites, and Catholics into their nationalistic ideological crusade.

These good people have been seduced, like the Amrights, into giving their lives and resources to a vision not found within Scripture—erecting a superstate for Jesus. They have confused promoting nationalism, militarism, and a narrow political agenda with advancing the kingdom of God. And some have elevated Rush Limbaugh to the status of the fourth person of the God . . . failing to note many of his views are diametrically in opposition to the testimonies of Jesus.

While we Christians are indeed called to be salt, light, and leaven in all areas, including the political, our primary mission is neither political or nationalistic. Our mission is to proclaim and demonstrate the good news of the gospel of Jesus Christ in partnership with Christians all over the world. And our mission has nothing to do with creating a U.S. superstate. Rather, we are called to work for the inbreaking of God's kingdom in every nation and culture. In other words, the establishment of God's kingdom isn't dependent on any nation, including the United States. God's movement is a transnational one.

When we do become politically involved, it is essential that we recognize that God's agenda transcends the ideological agendas of both the political right and the liberal left, of both Republicans and Democrats. Too many Christians have allowed a small elite right to define for them what it means to live responsibly in our changing world.

It is past time for conservative Christians to quit playing follow the leader and to begin reading both the newspaper and the Bible for themselves again. If we do that, we will discover we can't restrict our areas of biblical responsibility to the narrow nationalistic agenda of the religious right. The Bible speaks forcefully and often of God's concern for the poor and for social justice and peacemaking. The care of God's good creation and the call for people from different races and cultures to be reconciled in Jesus Christ are also strong biblical themes. Yet the religious right rarely addresses these issues because they don't fit their rightwing ideology.

And conservative Christians need a wake up call. Abortion is not the only issue or the only prolife issue. 40,000 children dying each day in the third world of hunger is a prolife issue! And children dying of gun violence in America is a prolife issue too! And God also cares very deeply about the growing and urgent poverty of children in the U.S.

We Christians dare not allow our lives and service to be

driven by fear, hysteria, and conspiracy fantasies of the right. Out of fear, many on the religious right resort to name calling, character assassination, and animosity, never looking for common ground with those with whom they disagree. If we are to be biblical Christians we must disavow the politics of polarization, and reach out to those with whom we differ in a spirit of love and reconciliation in Jesus Christ . . . learning to listen as well as share our views.

If we are going to create a life we can love, we must begin by setting aside many of the half-truths and false stories with which we have been raised. Many, like the Hightowers, many are beginning seriously to question whether pursuing ever more consumptive lifestyles of the Land of Evermore is the good life after all. And deep down, I think we all realize that radical individualism and "doing what's best for ourselves first" won't lead to satisfying living either. Nor will the contradictory visions of working for Fat City and waiting for soul rescue. And there is simply no biblical basis for seeking to promote a super state for Jesus.

To find a vision that not only makes a difference in our lives but in God's world, we must go back to the Bible. And we must ask a single question of Scripture: "What are God's purposes for the human future?"

The only way we can discern God's purposes for the future is to bring Scripture to bear not only on our relationship to God and others, but also on our fundamental aspirations. If we can discern something of God's purposes for the future, then we can discern a new sense of purpose and direction for our own lives. Then and only then can we create a way of life that we will truly love . . . and that will make a difference in God's world.

FOR THOUGHT AND DISCUSSION

None of the above stories fully match any reader's life situation. But let's discuss the following questions:

1. Which of the values or images in these stories are a part of your life and story? Do you identify with a particular couple? Do you find yourself defending a couple? Why?

2. What is the better future you want to achieve for yourself and your loved ones?
3. If you are in a group, try role playing the four different couples introduced in this chapter, advocating from their viewpoint the future you want for yourself and your family.

Joining the
stress-race to the land of Evermore

life direction	linkages	consequences
We Americans are raised, like the Hightowers, to believe that we will find the better future in joining the stress-race to the Land of Evermore. The upscale aspirations of the American Dream have become the aspirations of Christians and non-Christians alike. Our fundamental direction is defined largely by our drive to get ahead in our careers and communities.	We chose to link our lives to upwardly mobile aspirations because our families, friends and even churches insist that this is the road to the Land of Evermore. Remarkably few Christian leaders question if this dream is the dream for God's world.	In this scenario we have confused making a living with making a life. We have confused consumerism, individualism, and materialism with happiness. Belatedly we are discovering that the rat race isn't the good life after all. It is a fraudulent way up. And we are paying a high price in our own spiritual, physical, and mental lives and in our intimate relationships to God and others.

LIFE LINKS

Doing what's best for MYSELF _FIRST_

life direction	linkages	consequences
Some Christians, often in mainline churches, not only want to travel to the Land of Evermore, they also want to build an escalator into the dream to enable the poor to get a little taste of Evermore too. But a number of Christians have added a new dimension to the dream . . . not only material comfort but personal freedom and self actualization. And a new radical form of autonomy has emerged. "I have to do what's best for myself first."	Instead of questioning the fundamental aspirations of the dream, many Mainliners have also linked their lives rather thoughtlessly to its fulfillment. They simply want to see the dream operate a little more justly as long as it does not cost too much. Added to this is an unexamined linking of life, by many, to a radical autonomy that elevates personal well-being and personal choice above virtually all responsibilities and relationships in human community.	Not only do Mainliners pay the same price as everyone else because of buying into the rat race. . . . Those who buy into radical autonomy pay an additional high price in fractured relationships, diminished community, and the creation of individualistic, egocentric lifestyles.

LIFE LINKS

Waiting for Soul Rescue and working for Fat City

life direction	linkages	consequences
Many evangelicals and charismatics seem to hold two different visions for the future that really aren't compatible. On the one hand many of us look forward to the future of God as a non-material existence in the clouds. In the meantime many evangelicals and charismatics are not only working as hard as anyone else to get to Fat City . . . they believe that getting a big piece of the consumer pie is proof of their spirituality.	Many have linked to two very different visions for the future and have not recognized that not only are the visions inherently contradictory, but neither is biblical.	Focusing on an escape to a non-materialistic existence in the clouds has caused many evangelicals and charismatics to disengage from working for social change today. At the same time, their unquestioned commitment to Fat City is pulling many away from sharing their resources with others. Both visions tend to cause conservative Christians to become more self-centered in both their piety and their upscale lifestyles.

LIFE LINKS

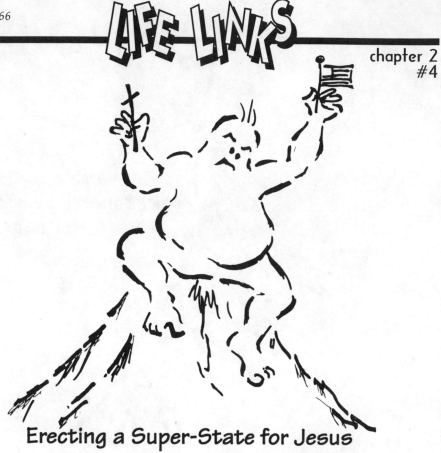

Erecting a Super-State for Jesus

life direction	linkages	consequences
Some on the religious right have adopted a vision of messianic nationalism. They believe God has somehow chosen the United States to be his agent on earth—working as a nation to carry out his purposes. Therefore the task of Christians is to take America back from a humanist take over in order to head off the establishment of a godless one world government.	Conservative Christians who link their lives to this vision of messianic nationalism are sincere. But while claiming to be people of the Book, they don't seem to recognize that there is no biblical material to support the view that the United States has been chosen by God to replace his church as his agent on earth.	This vision of the better future tends to "baptize Americanism and politicize the church"—to create a new civil religion that seriously departs from a biblical faith. More tragically, it draws lives and resources of believers away from proclaiming and demonstrating the gospel of Jesus Christ to support a very narrow political agenda.

Connecting with the Story of God

onnecting! Deep within every person is a longing to be connected to a story larger than ourselves. We sense it isn't enough simply to buy into the stories that make up our small world—stories we have discovered are often filled with distortions, illusions, and half-truths. Even when we invest every ounce of energy scaling the illusory peaks these stories call us to, they end up disappointing us. As we have discovered, even some of our religious stories are inadequate.

At the very center of our beings we sense there is something more . . . a different way up. We want our lives to count for something. And the only way we are going to get there is to connect our lives to a dream bigger than we are—a dream big enough for the times and the world in which we live. We will find that connection only when we merge our lives and our stories with the story of God.

The intent of this chapter then is to enable you to relive the panoramic study of God in order to discover God's loving purposes for our lives and God's world . . . to help us find a new way up.

But why all this emphasis on "story"—especially "the story of God"? Only as we begin to comprehend the Story of God in its entirety and something of the Creator God's loving purposes for us can we find direction for our lives and congregations. The God who made us knows that a story is one of the best ways for us to connect with truths larger than ourselves.

Garrison Keillor, famed for sharing engaging yarns on the National Public Radio, has helped us understand the compelling power of stories to connect us with the larger world. His homely recollections of his mythical hometown of Lake Wobegon, Minnesota, somehow remind us of our common past, the poignancy of the everyday and the seasons of our lives. For example,

> The Sons of Knute Ice Melt Contest starts on Groundhog Day, when they tow Mr. Gerge's maroon 1949 Ford onto the lake, park it forty yards off shore with a long chain around the rear axle and wait for spring. You guess the day and the hour she will go down, at a dollar per guess. The winner gets a boat, and the profits go to the Sons of Knute Shining Start Scholarship Fund to send kids to college. . . .
>
> The first week of April is a good guess, though the car has sunk as early as late March and as late as the third week of April. Once it never went down. They parked it off the end of the long sandbar that comes off the point. The Ford sat there in four inches of water, a sort of buoy, and the scholarship fund earned hundreds of dollars. . . .
>
> On the first real warm day, you can sit on the back steps in your P.J.s before church, drink coffee, study the backyard, which was such a dump a week ago you wouldn't have wanted to be buried there, but with the tulips coming up and a faint haze on the lilacs, a person can see this is not the moon but earth, a planet named for its finely ground rock containing organic material that, given sunlight and moisture, can produce plant life and many support advanced life forms such as Catholics and Lutherans. School windows open and faint wisps of talk drift out and choral music. Rototillers start up, and the first whap of a ball in a glove is heard . . .
>
> On the first real warm Sunday, attendance is down at church, people deciding God being everywhere they can worship him

anywhere—what Fr. Emil calls "the Protestant fallacy." He strolls around after mass, surprising some absentees who were busy worshiping with rakes and didn't see him coming.[1]

As Garrison Keillor spins his tale, we find ourselves getting involved, reconnecting with the smells, tastes, and renewal of spirit that come with the thawing of winter and arrival of spring. I am convinced that is the way we need to connect with the Creator and God's story of redemption.

Reconnecting with the Story

But of course we're talking about a story grander than springtime in Minnesota! We're talking about something large enough to live and die for.

Growing up in northern California, I quickly learned that when people in my part of the state said they were going to "the city," they meant San Francisco—even though there were other cities nearby. In the same way, although there are many stories that seek to explain the human experience and to describe the human future (we've looked at a few of them), the epic of God is in a class by itself. Its sweep ranges from creation to consummation and remarkably includes your life and mine.

Now in referring to God's acts in history as a "story," I am not suggesting they aren't true! I hold a high view of Scripture. However, it is important to recognize that faith does not come to us first as "theology"—as a set of systematic precepts. No, our faith comes to us as a story—The Story. The crisis the North American church is facing is that we have lost both our story and our vision for the future. In "losing the story," Robert McAfee Brown insists, "we have lost both the power and the glory. We have committed the unpardonable sin of transforming exciting stories into dull systems. We must recover The Story if we are to have a faith for our day." [2]

What has caused this crisis? I believe we have not taken seriously the story of God or Christian Scripture. Conservative Christians pride themselves on maintaining a high view of Scripture, but the irony and the tragedy is that they often apply

Scripture only to a small spiritual compartment of their lives. They bring Scripture to bear on their relationships to God and each other and on inner healing, and that is important. Mennonites, Catholics, and mainline Protestants also bring Scripture to bear on socioeconomic and political issues, and that too is important.

However, rarely do I find Christians of any stripe who bring Scripture to bear on the fundamental aspirations that drive our lives or the values on which our lives are premised. We allow the secular culture to define not only the direction of our lives but also what we value.

If we really want to find a new way up, we need to go back to the Bible asking a single question: "What are God's purposes for the human future?" If we can discover within Scripture something of God's purposes for the future, then we can then gain a new sense of direction for our lives, a new definition of the "good life."

We can discover in the story of God a vision for our lives vastly superior to simply pursuing the American Dream with a little Jesus overlay and all the other aspirations we looked at in the last chapter.

Welcome to the Drama of God

Perhaps it's easiest to visualize this Story as a vast drama—spanning all history. Picture the incredible range of locations—from the awesome pyramids of Egypt to the rugged magnificence of Mount Sinai; from Jerusalem's teeming streets to Rome's luxurious imperial palace. Nothing can match this epic for pure panoramic sweep. It is more variegated and compelling than any other human drama—filled with stories of heroism, romance, tragedy, comedy, rebellion, and restoration.

Christopher Wright helpfully breaks this enormous drama down into nine segments. His outline can serve as a useful guide as we re-live the drama of The Story of God from opening curtain to the dimming of the final footlights.

Act 1: The Creation
Act 2: The Fall
Act 3: The Call of Abraham and Sarah
Act 4: The Exodus Experience and the Creation of the People of
    the Covenant
Act 5: The Life and Ministry of the Messiah
Act 6: The Crucifixion and Resurrection of Jesus
Act 7: Pentecost and the Church Age
Act 8: The Return of Christ
Act 9: The Creation of a New Heaven and a New Earth[3]

As you can see from this outline, The Story doesn't conclude at the end of the first century A.D. with the writings of the apostles. This story, because it is *The* Story, stretches across the ages and centuries, through your life and mine, and into the unfinished future. We are living in the middle of Act 7—between Pentecost and the return of Christ.

Given this perspective, you and I have an important role in this drama. Like it or not, we are called on to be a part of The Story of God. As John Dunne suggests about the stories of the New Testament,

> Perhaps the special character of the stories . . . lies in the fact that they are not told for themselves, that they are not only about other people, but that they are always about us. They locate us in the very midst of the great story and plot of all time and space, and therefore relate us to the great dramatist and story teller, God himself.[4]

To play out our role in God's drama, however, we must understand the drama's direction and character. We must understand the intentions of the Playwright for a people and a world.

Picture yourself as not only a member of the audience for this epic production but also one of the actors. You are both viewing and participating in all we are going to experience together. Pay particular attention to God's loving purposes revealed in this drama, because they will inform us as to our role when it is our turn in the footlights.

Prepare for the opening scene.

Watch in hushed silence.

Act One . . . In the Beginning

Act one, scene one. No props, no stage, no earth, no life. Nothing. In the darkness, we hear those words ringing through space and time: "In the beginning, God."

"In the beginning God created the heavens and the earth. And the earth was formless and void, and darkness was over the surface of the deep; and the Spirit of God was moving over the surface of the waters. Then God said, 'let there be light' " (Gen. 1:1-3). And the lights come up and the majestic spectacle of creation takes place before our very eyes.

We find ourselves in a lavish, beautiful garden. All around we see the loving intentions of the Creator. We experience a world of rhythmic night and day, darkness and light—a world of spectacular variety, color, and sound, with birds piercing the heavens and fish filling the sea.

The evidence from Scripture is abundant that "the earth is the Lord's and the fulness thereof, the world and those who dwell therein" (Ps. 24:1). Also, "the heavens are telling the glory of God; and the firmament proclaims his handiwork" (Ps. 19:1). Throughout both the Old and New Testaments we find hymns affirming the goodness and the glory of God's creation. And we the image bearers of the Creator God are appointed stewards of this good creation.

Act Two . . . The Fatal Choice

One solitary light comes up slowly on two people attempting to hide themselves in foliage. We see terror and anguish etched on their shadowed faces. We immediately identify with what they are feeling—the hiding, the alienation, and the apprehension. We find ourselves drawn into this disturbing scene, and we all know what happened.

Our forebears, a man and a woman, not content to walk with their Maker in the cool of the garden, decide to rewrite the script, to try their hand at directing the drama and their own lives. And the consequences are disastrous; everything is disrupted. Tragically, not only is the couple alienated from their

Creator, but creation itself becomes tragically twisted.

You see, the consequences of the Fall are much more far-reaching than many Christians recognize. Humankind does indeed become alienated from God as a direct consequence of the Fall. But the alienation is not just spiritual! We humans become corrupted in every area of our lives. Physically, we become subject to disease, decay, and death. Intellectually, we become driven by the lust to know as God knows and to be powerful as God is powerful. We learn to rationalize our evil. Our minds become darkened, and our arrogance grows.

At every level—including family, sexual, parental, societal, and international—human relationships are fractured and disrupted by the Fall. The earth itself has fallen under the curse because of human sin. As a consequence, we humans find ourselves in a constant life-and-death struggle with the larger environment. And sin and evil become not only personal, but corporate and societal, permeating the entire created order.

So how can this fallen creation be redeemed? Christopher Wright accurately points out that the remedy must match the disease. If the malady of sin has corrupted not only our spiritual lives but also our personal, relational, and global interactions, then we need a cure as comprehensive as the sickness.

Obviously a divine initiative interested only in rescuing people's souls will be totally inadequate for such a task.[5] We need a redemptive remedy that restores broken bodies, reconciles broken relationships, and labors for the renewal of this good creation by the power of the living God. That's a tall order.

Act Three . . . A New Initiative

Let's see what the Playwright does to mount a new initiative, to address the comprehensive corruption of humanity and distortion of creation. As the curtain rises on act three, the hot desert sun is bearing down on us through clouds of dust stirred up by the caravan we seem to be a part of—sheep, goats, heavy laden camels, and dozens of people on foot. They are heading for a distant oasis. An older couple leads this ragged parade.

What good can God possibly achieve through this small

band? It soon becomes a little clearer. For this group is traveling on a promise! They are on the move because God has spoken to their aged leader in words of calling and words of promise, bidding him to leave his home in a thriving city and go into a distant land he has never seen.

God has promised Abraham and Sarah a new future containing the seeds of the promise of a new humanity and a new creation. Yahweh has promised that all the peoples of the earth will be blessed through this one couple and their offspring (see Gen. 12:3).

In this act of God's story, Yahweh takes a surprising initiative to restore relationship with humankind by establishing a covenant with Abraham, Sarah, and their descendants.

> This new history requires a wrenching departure, an abandonment of what is, for that which is not, but which is promised by the One who will do what He says. "And he went!" Sarah was barren! No way to the future. No heir to receive all the riches. Nothing. Future closed off. Everything as good as over and done with. And He spoke and there was newness. The family of Abraham left the history of expulsion and began the pilgrimage of promise.[6]

Unbelievably, God establishes this new covenant to restore the human future with a ninety-year-old couple. The Playwright bets the entire play on their faith and their obedience. But how in the world is the Creator God going to make their descendants more numerous than the stars and bless the world—when Sarah has never had a child and in the declining years of life?

The lights go up on the next scene; an ancient woman is in the middle of the stage, laughing uproariously.

> She is an old woman, and, after a life time in the desert, her face is cracked and rutted like a six-month drought. She hunches her shoulders around her ears and starts to shake. She squinnies her eyes shut and her laughter is all china teeth and wheeze and tears running down as she rocks back and forth in her kitchen chair. She is laughing because she is pushing ninety-one and has

just been told she is going to have a baby. Even though it was an angel who told her, she can't control herself, and her husband can't control himself either. He keeps a straight face a few seconds longer than she does, but he ends up cracking up too. Even the angel is not unaffected. He hides his mouth behind his golden scapular, but you can still see his eyes. They are larkspur blue and brimming with something of which the laughter of the old woman and her husband is at best only a rough translation.

The old woman's name is Sarah, of course, and the old man's name is Abraham, and they are laughing at the idea of a baby being born in the geriatric ward and Medicare's picking up the tab.

She was hiding behind the tent door when the angel spoke, and it was her laughter that got them all going. According to Genesis, God intervened then and asked about Sarah's laughter, and Sarah scared stiff denied the whole thing. Then God said, "No, but you did laugh," and of course he was right. Maybe the most interesting part of it all is that far from getting angry at them for laughing, God told them that when the baby was born He wanted them to name him Isaac, which in Hebrew means laughter.[7]

Only a playwright with an outrageous sense of humor, or a Creator God committed to redeeming history through the unlikely, would choose a couple on the verge of needing nursing home care to start a new nation! It certainly wasn't typecasting. How like God, though, to begin this new initiative with impossibilities and with laughter!

Act Four . . . A New Freedom

After an intermission in which everyone dries their eyes and regains their composure, we return to our seats for the fourth act. The room darkens.

In the distance the huge sun slowly descends, swallowed by the overwhelming darkness of the night. Silhouetted are the shapes of huge temples, sculptured forms, and pyramids. In the foreground, a thousand slaves are dragging massive stones toward a construction site. The noise, the humidity, the smells are almost overpowering.

An overseer's rod smashes down on the back of a crippled

slave, driving him to the ground, his own blood running down his arms. A growing number of slaves undergo the whip as the sun retires behind the temple, plunging us into a darkness much deeper than before. The groans from the fallen also fade; we are engulfed in a mysterious silence.

It seems as though we have been in the darkness and silence forever, when suddenly an anguished scream pierces the night. Then again there is silence.

Finally one small child emerges from the shadows before us. He is in a small hut with his family, and a single spotlight focuses on him. He just stands there looking at us quizzically.

"Why is this night different from every other night?" he asks. "Every other night we eat both leavened and unleavened bread. Why do we eat only the unleavened bread tonight?"

A voice booms out from the back, "Tonight is different because this is the night the angel of the Lord passed over the house of Israel." The voice goes on to describe the miracles that resulted in the liberation of the children of Israel from the bondage of Egypt.

Then the lights go up as unleavened bread, bitter herbs, salted water are passed and the celebration of the Passover begins. Music starts abruptly in the wings and everyone spontaneously begins to dance the Hora. The air fills with the joy of liberation, festivity, and hope as we experience together the deliverance of God's people from bondage. Within us a hope for the future begins to stir as well.

The Jewish people have long understood the importance of telling one another their story through celebration, dancing, and singing. Every Passover they relive their miraculous deliverance from captivity.

God's redemptive intent from the beginning was to create a new people. And even as God chose an unlikely couple to parent a nation, God selected "a people who were not people" to carry out God's redemptive purposes in the world. The Creator God chose an unlikely, despised group of Semite slaves—descendants of Abraham—to be the people of God. As Moses lead them to Mount Sinai they entered into covenant with their liberator God.

In the story of the Exodus, we are forcefully reminded that God's loving intentions are not just spiritual but political, economic, and social as well. God ever stands against oppression on the side of the oppressed, of those seeking deliverance and justice. In fact the future promised the children of Israel is "a land flowing with milk and honey."

Of course you know how the story goes. The children of Israel, under Moses' leadership, don't immediately enter the Promised Land once they have left bondage in Egypt. Instead they wander forty years in a wasteland as landless refugees, because of their chronically disobedient and recalcitrant behavior.

But God never gives up and never wavers from God's redemptive purposes. Later God gives them the Ten Commandments to guide their behavior. Always, as Brueggemann reminds us, "He is there with Israel. He subjects himself to the same circumstances as Israel. He also sojourns without rootage, with his people en route to the fulfilling land of Promise." [8]

Countless followers in ages since have made this wilderness story theirs. Too well we have all known the bitter grief of our sin. Too often we have longed for "the leeks and garlics" of our former life. But like the children of Israel, we are led patiently on by our God, who refuses to give up on us and is determined to transport us safely to the promised future.

Finally one bright morning, after years of disobedience and compromise, we reach the crest of Mt. Nebo and look down on the Promised Land. As that landscape flowing with milk and honey stretches before us, the goodness of God overwhelms us.

The pure radical grace of God in giving God's people a homeland is a foretaste of the Creator's loving homecoming for all people. God's promise to Abraham, Isaac, and Jacob is fulfilled.

> For the Lord your God is bringing you into a good land, a land of brooks of water, of fountains and springs, flowing forth in valleys and hills, a land of wheat and barley, of vines and fig trees and pomegranates, a land of olive trees and honey, a land in which you will eat bread without scarcity, in which you will lack nothing, a land whose stones are iron, and out of whose hills you can dig copper. And you shall eat and be full, and you shall

bless the Lord your God for the good land he has given you
(Deut. 8:7-10, RSV).

This is our story too. This is a foretaste of all God intends—to
bring the redeemed people of the Lord from all generations
home to the goodness and mercy of God.

Of course, act four of God's story doesn't end when the children of Israel reach the Promised Land. There are scenes of
courtly splendor as they form a kingdom (a foreshadowing of
the coming of God's transcendent kingdom) and King David
leads them to pinnacles of influence and power. And during the
reign of Solomon new cities are constructed, the kingdom is ex-
panded, and a temple is erected in Jerusalem for the worship of
the living God.

There are also scenes of failure, disappointment, and judgment. God's people repeatedly turn from the Creator and fall
into sin. Again and again the voices of the prophets are heard
above scenes of idolatry, oppression, and immorality with their
warnings of God's judgment.

The message of the prophets to the people of Israel is that
God's goodness to them isn't automatic but based on their obedience and faithfulness. When the people fail to heed the
prophets, judgment comes. The lights come up on a weary line
of Hebrews trudging their way toward captivity in Babylon.
What was foretold by the prophets has tragically come to pass.

God's judgment of the children of Israel comes for three major reasons: idolatry, sexual immorality, and oppression of the
poor. But many evangelicals only acknowledge the first two. I
have heard any number of sermons about God's judgment on
his people for idolatry and sexual immorality. But I rarely hear
sermons ready to declare that God judges those who oppress
and exploit the poor. Most evangelicals I talk with know Sodom
was judged for sexual sins, but they are surprised to learn
Sodom was also judged for mistreatment of the poor: "Behold,
this was the guilt of your sister Sodom: she and her daughters
had arrogance, abundant food, and careless ease, but she did
not help the poor and needy" (Ezek. 16:49, NASB).

But the prophets' message is not only one of judgment.

While Isaiah, Jeremiah, and Amos declare God's anger, they also offer compelling hope that God's redemptive purposes will one day be achieved—that the day of the Lord will come. Listen to the ringing words of the prophet Isaiah.

> The people who walked in darkness have seen a great light: light has dawned upon them, dwellers in a land as dark as death. Thou hast increased their joy and given them great gladness. . . . For thou hast shattered the yoke that burdened them, the collar that lay heavy on their shoulders, the driver's goad, as on the day of Midian's defeat. All the boots of trampling soldiers and the garments fouled with blood shall become a burning mass, fuel for fire. For a boy has been born to us, a son given to us to bear the symbol of dominion on his shoulder; and he shall be called in purpose wonderful, in battle God-like, Father for all time, Prince of peace. Great shall the dominion be, and boundless the peace bestowed on David's throne and on his kingdom, to establish it and sustain it with justice and righteousness from now and for evermore. (Isa. 9:2-7, NEB)

Act Five . . . A New Compassion

There is a long silence after the fourth act of God's story— four hundred years of silence and anticipation. But finally the footlights come up as we begin the fifth act.

A white-haired figure is signaling to a group of friends, using the animated gestures of one who cannot speak. Finally in frustration he picks up a slate and begins to write. Then the old man abruptly throws down the slate and shouts, in a voice hoarse from months of disuse, the words he has just written: "His name is John!"

And Zacharias goes on to speak these exuberant words of praise to celebrate the birth of his newborn son, foretold to him by an angel.

> Blessed be the Lord God of Israel, for He has visited us and accomplished redemption for His people, and has raised up a horn of salvation for us in the house of David His servant—as He spoke by the mouth of His holy prophets from of old—salvation from our enemies, and from the hand of all who hate us; to show mercy toward our fathers, and to remember His holy covenant,

the oath which He swore to Abraham our father, to grant us that we, being delivered from the hand of our enemies, might serve Him without fear, in holiness and righteousness before Him all our days.

And you, child, will be called the prophet of the Most High; for you will go on before the Lord to prepare His ways; to give to His people the knowledge of salvation by the forgiveness of their sins, because of the tender mercy of our God, with which the Sunrise from on high shall visit us, to shine upon those who sit in darkness and the shadow of death, to guide our feet into the way of peace. (Luke 1:68-79, NASB)

Now the light on Zacharias dims and comes up on a young woman upstage. She is on her knees, her arms lifted toward heaven; her words, too, ring out with praise:

My soul exalts the Lord, and my spirit has rejoiced in God my Savior. For He has had regard for the humble state of His bondslave; for behold, from this time on all generations will count me blessed. For the Mighty One has done great things for me; and holy is His name, and His mercy is upon generation after generation towards those who fear Him. He has done mighty deeds with His arm; He has scattered those who were proud in the thoughts of their heart. He has brought down rulers from their thrones, and has exalted those who were humble. He has filled the hungry with good things; and sent away the rich empty-handed. He has given help to Israel His servant, in remembrance of His mercy, as He spoke to our fathers, to Abraham and his offspring forever. (vv. 46-55, NASB)

These are words not only announcing the loving intervention of the Creator God in history, but restating God's loving intentions. Certainly these include forgiveness from sin and mercy for those who serve God in righteousness, but they don't stop there. God's redemptive initiative will have an impact on every dimension of human experience—not only the spiritual, but the social, political, and economic as well. The one who is coming will turn everything right side up.

Zacharias expects God's new initiative to mean political liberation from those who had oppressed God's people. And

Mary sees God's redemptive initiative as totally reordering human society—pulling down the powerful and influential from their pinnacles and promoting the nobodies; unburdening the affluent of their wealth, and giving good things to the hungry, the powerless, the impoverished.

It is clear in both these visions that God's redemptive intent is not just the conversion of sinners but the transformation of *everything.* As David Bosch insists

> When redemption is confined to man's [and woman's] personal relationship to God, when somebody is saved but all his relationships remain unaffected, when structural and institutional sins are not exposed, we are involved with an unbiblical one-sidedness and a spurious Christianity.[9]

But we must return to our play—for the spotlight has shifted again. The scene now before us is so familiar that at first we don't notice how surprising it really is! God's redemptive initiatives comes to us in unlikely ways—a senior citizen gives birth to a son named "Laughter," or a nation of obstinate refugee slaves is chosen as God's people. But now opens the unlikeliest scene of all—a man and a woman struggle to bring life into the world . . . in a cow stall. And who shows up at this historic birth? Not the religious leaders but a band of poor shepherds.

Now the scenes are shifting quickly. We move to a little town called Nazareth some years later. The infant has become a man. Raised in a small Jewish village, trained as a carpenter and not a teacher, he nevertheless stands up on the Sabbath in the synagogue to read. He is handed the book of the prophet Isaiah.

> And He opened the book, and found the place where it was written, "The Spirit of the Lord is upon Me, because He anointed Me to preach the gospel to the poor. He has sent Me to proclaim release to the captives, and recovery of sight to the blind, to set free those who are downtrodden, to proclaim the favorable year of the Lord." And He closed the book, and gave it back to the attendant, and sat down; and the eyes of all in the synagogue were fixed upon Him. And He began to say to them, "Today this Scripture has been fulfilled in your hearing." (Luke 4:17-21, NASB)

What does he mean, "Today the Scripture has been fulfilled in your hearing"? What exactly is the significance of his reading this Scripture? It is the inauguration of Jesus' ministry. He is not only announcing his vocation—devoting his life to working for the purposes of God. He is also announcing that God's loving future is breaking into our midst. And he calls others to follow him in devoting their lives to working for God's purposes.

Connecting with the Story of God

Jesus Christ comes not only announcing the inbreaking of God's kingdom but demonstrating it. He is God's future made present. Every time Jesus hears a man who has never walked before . . . and that man dances down the street praising God . . . we are given a glimpse of God's future. Every time Jesus feeds the hungry, forgives the sinner, hugs the kids, we are given a preview of coming attractions. In Jesus Christ, the future of God has broken into our world at the initiative of a Creator who is intent on making all things new.

When John sends his followers to ask whether Jesus is the Messiah or not, Jesus responds in language similar to his Nazareth inaugural, "Go back and report to John what you have seen and heard: The blind receive sight, the lame walk, those who have leprosy are cured, the deaf hear, the dead are raised, and the good news is preached to the poor. Blessed is the man who does not fall away on account of me" (Luke 7:22-23, NIV).

Quite simply what it meant for Jesus to be the Messiah of God was to devote his life to working for the purposes of God . . . preaching good news to the poor, proclaiming release to the captives, recovery of sight to the blind and set free the oppressed. And those first disciples understood if they were to follow Jesus they not only needed to commit their lives to God but to working for the purposes of God just as he did. Even as Jesus was a man for others they became a people for others . . . extending God's love by word and deed. They found a new way up.

One of the first things Jesus did was to start a new community that was not only devoted to working for the purposes of God but was also committed to reflecting something of the values of God's new order. As they began to reorder their lives around the purposes of God they did outrageous things like quitting jobs and leaving homes. They found a new reason for being in the world.

Those first disciples discovered that following Christ not only radically transformed their lives but also the character of their existence. They became an incarnational foretaste of the celebrative future of God as they healed the sick, welcomed the outcast, and fleshed out the right-side-up values of the kingdom in an upside-down world. The world will never be the same.

Act Six . . . A New Sacrifice

When the curtain goes up this time, we are all ushered on stage. We find ourselves pushed in a human crush down the narrow twisting back streets of Jerusalem.

Soldiers everywhere watch from windows and doorways. The crowd surges past us. Shouts. Raised fists. Parents carrying children. Others carrying scaffolding. Centurions push us forcefully into a doorway, almost knocking us down, blocking our view.

The unruly crowd eventually dwindles and passes. We follow. The skies darken. Huge colonnades of clouds gather on the horizon as the crowd clusters on a barren knoll just outside the city gates.

It's difficult to see what's happening from back here. It looks as if they are beginning a construction project on the knoll. Beams and timbers—workmen and soldiers. A small group of women, heads covered, quickly press past us, making their way to the small dark hill.

As one huge beam is lifted upright, silhouetted against the blackening sky, the chattering and movement abruptly stop. All eyes are fixed on the hilltop.

Everything is in frozen frame for what seems like forever. The only motion is that of the encroaching clouds. The biting wind whips our legs. We stand as one person, transfixed in uncomprehending silence.

Suddenly an anguished voice rises above the hilltop and throng. "My God, my God, why have you forsaken me?" Then all is dark and silent.

Godforsakenness, torturous suffering, humiliating death. He has taken the bitter cup and drunk it down to the dregs. There was no holding back. Jesus has tasted it all.

Jesus knows the overwhelming sense of abandonment that a five-year-old child is experiencing on a garbage dump in Manila. He knows the despair of a farmer in Chad watching his family slowly die of malnutrition. He knows the hopelessness of a college student in Chicago who learns his recently discovered malignancy is terminal. Jesus has experienced it all.

And the Creator and Author of this story, through the abandonment, suffering, and death of the Son, has tasted it all too. Our God is not untouched by our infirmities; God in Christ experienced them all. And as the Creator God enters fully into our stories, God experiences anew our suffering, pain, and sense of abandonment.

As we go on to the next scene, everything remains in darkness. All is deadly quiet, stifling. Still echoing in our minds is that last terrible cry: "My God, my God. . . ."

Suddenly we realize we are no longer bystanders. We are there—with Jesus' disciples, tasting their hopelessness. We have given up our livelihoods, traveled from village to village. We had thought he was the one. Now he's dead, and it's as though we died with him. It's over; we have entered a despair darker than the night which engulfs us. It's almost as if we are there with him in the silent, dark crypt.

Dear God, why have you forsaken us?

Then, after what seems like an eternity, we hear a sound, a faint sound at first—stone against stone. A brilliant ray of light blinds us. As we are struggling to adjust our eyes a hand takes ours.

As we enter daylight with our resurrected Lord, we are struck by the realization that on this side of the empty tomb there is no basis for despair, since the God of resurrection promises to make all things new.

For our God has not only experienced all godforsakenness,

suffering, pain, and death through Jesus Christ; the God of history has put an end to them. God has defeated the crushing works of darkness and, in so doing, reconciled all things to God's self.

Remember, we said at the beginning of the chapter that everything as ruptured in the Fall must be set right in the kingdom. That is exactly what God has done through the crucifixion and the resurrection of Jesus. Christ's death and resurrection have reconciled us to our God. In that merciful act, as we embrace it as our own, we are made new. Our sins are forgiven, and we are adopted into the family of God.

"Once you were alienated from God and were enemies in your minds because of your evil behavior," Paul wrote to the Colossians. "But now he has reconciled you by Christ's physical body through death to present you holy in his sight" (Col. 1:22, NIV).

God acted in Christ to reconcile us not only to the Creator God but to one another as well. God is at work in history fashioning a new inclusive society of reconciliation, in which there will be no distinction based on race, culture, and gender. In this new messianic community, "there is neither Jew nor Greek, slave nor free, male nor female, for you are all one in Christ Jesus" (Gal. 3:28, NIV).

Finally, Christ's loving sacrifice and triumphant resurrection not only reconciles us to God and to one another, but also reconciles all things to him—including the entire created order. "For God was pleased to have all his fullness dwell in him, and through him to reconcile to himself all things, whether things on earth or things in heaven, by making peace through his blood, shed on the cross" (Col. 1:19-20, NIV).

Jurgen Moltmann reminds us that the brutal cross is also our doorway to a future made new. "God suffered in the suffering of Jesus, God died on the cross of Christ, says Christian faith, so that we might live and rise again in his future."[10]

The resurrection not only has implications for our personal lives and the community of Jesus in the world today; it is our pledge for tomorrow, as well. The resurrection of Jesus is the pledge that all God promised in the final act of his drama will come to pass—that we, too, will be resurrected to live with the Creator forever in a new heaven and earth.

After the resurrection of Jesus, his followers jubilantly regrouped. Dismay, despair, and confusion melted away. Faith and hope reignited. Followers spent a forty-day crash course on the kingdom of God with their risen Lord. And his last word to them was to wait in Jerusalem for the coming of the Spirit. They did. And they were not disappointed.

Act Seven . . . A New Community

As the lights go up on the next act, we find we are still onstage—in Jerusalem. People everywhere. Color and spectacle. The Jewish feast day of Pentecost. Jerusalem bulging at the seams with travelers from around the world. We struggle through the press of animals and people and come to a small building. While we climb the stairway, we hear urgent praying.

As we reach the doorway, a violent wind fills the house, turning everything upside down. Flames of fire appear over the heads of those who are praying. They are filled with the Spirit of God and begin speaking with other tongues. As we watch, those who were praying rush past us into the streets. Amazingly, others in the streets, from many different nations, hear people speaking their own languages.

Peter raises his voice above the din,

> Men of Israel, listen to this: Jesus of Nazareth was a man accredited by God to you by miracles, wonders and signs, which God did among you through him, as you yourselves know. This man was handed over to you by God's set purpose and foreknowledge; and you, with the help of wicked men, put him to death by nailing him to the cross. But God raised him from the dead, freeing him from the agony of death, because it was impossible for death to keep its hold on him." (Acts 2:22-24, NIV)

People are cut in their hearts and many turn to God. Three thousand are baptized on this remarkable day.

With the coming of the Spirit a new movement is born. At first it was really a movement of messianic Judaism. But even on that first day there are clear signs that the messianic community of Jesus is going to be an international movement bursting the wineskins of traditional Judaism. Soon Peter learns that even Gentiles can follow the Messiah. And the movement begins to change. The promise to Abraham and Sarah really does begin to become true all over the planet.

From the first act of this drama it has been clear that God intended to create a people for God's self—a new community. That is what God has given us at the feast of Pentecost, a new community. And as we will see later, this community is radically different from the world around it; it is a living foretaste of the promised future of God.

That brings us almost to the end of the story as told in the Bible. But as I have said, God's Story doesn't end there. Act seven of God's Story continues through the ages into the present day. In the next chapter we will look at some compelling scenes of how other disciples have committed their lives to the purposes of God just like those first disciples did.

But first, I want to look ahead to acts eight and nine as they are described to us in Scripture. For as we look ahead to the final fulfillment of God's promises, we will see how widely God's Story differs from the small stories and the superficial dreams to which we have given our lives. In God's Story we find a celebrative new dream that calls us beyond ourselves. . . . That offers us a new way up.

Acts Eight and Nine . . . A New Creation

As the curtain goes up, we see a huge mountain stretching out of sight into the clouds. People are streaming to it from all directions. We, too, leave our seats and begin to move toward the mountain of the Lord.

The barren landscape begins to give way to lush olive groves. Pomegranates and citrus line the path. And even as the barrenness around us gives way to exuberant life, the same transformation begins to happen within us. It's almost as though our vision is being radically corrected.

Starting up the gigantic mountain, we find abandoned

wheelchairs and crutches discarded along the side of the trail. Singing, dancing, and celebration sweep through the crowd. Arm in arm we go up to the mountain together.

> How lovely on the mountains are the feet of him who brings good news, who announces peace and brings good news of happiness, who announces salvation, and says to Zion, "Your God reigns!" Listen! Your watchmen lift up their voices, they shout joyfully together; for they will see with their own eyes when the Lord restores Zion. Break forth, shout joyfully together, you waste places of Jerusalem; for the Lord has comforted His people, He has redeemed Jerusalem. The Lord has bared His holy arm in the sight of all the nations; that all the ends of the earth may see the salvation of our God. (Isa. 52:7-10, NASB)

As we continue our ascent, the throng begins to chant in a dozen different languages. "The Bridegroom is coming! The Bridegroom is coming! The Bridegroom is coming!" A huge canopy greets us as we reach the summit. It's festooned with ribbons, flowers, and palm branches. Filipinos, Arabs, Haitians, and a thousand others crowd in from all directions. The best that's ever been will be alive again!

> And I saw a new heaven and a new earth; for the first heaven and the first earth passed away, and there is no longer any sea. And I saw the holy city, new Jerusalem, coming down out of heaven from God, made ready as a bride adorned for her husband. (Rev. 21:1-2)

Listen to the unbridled joy a young Jew experienced on his wedding night and imagine how much more we can anticipate when the Bridegroom comes for his people.

> We met under the canopy. . . . The procession broke and crowded round us; all raising their candles high in the air. The Rabbi, his face radiant under the high pointed skull-cap, made us stand with our faces to the east, toward Jerusalem, the holy city, and began the sermon: "This, my children, is the most momentous hour of your lives."
> Beside me I felt the form of my bride. . . . "And as God's agent

on earth, you should know that all your being, all your life is dedicated to the purposes of the Almighty. . . . Remember, O bridegroom and bride, that you are going to be collaborators in the endless story of creation which begins in Genesis." The vows were exchanged. Someone put the bride's arm in mine and the musicians led the way, playing a tumultuous Cossack dance. Everything around me danced, the air, the candles, the very stars in the highest heaven. . . ."[11]

Of course the biblical images for acts eight and nine of God's story are not all ones of hilarity and celebration. As the prophets in act four warned, our God is a judge. And the earth is going to face a time of judgment for our personal and corporate sins. The earth will be purged with fire, and we will be judged by God for serving the false idols of our age, for personal immorality and materialism and our indifference to those in need.

The earth will go through the birth trauma of the judgment of God. But then will come the birth of God's new creation. Howard Snyder assures us,

Here we face the certainty and the mystery of the judgment. The earth will undergo a change, a refining fire, but it will not be annihilated! The whole creation will be set free (Romans 8:21). As with our bodies so with the earth: "The perishable must clothe itself with the imperishable." (1 Corinthians 15:33)[12]

A Different Dream . . . God's Present and Coming Kingdom

I am sure we have seen enough by now to realize that God's Story and God's dream for the future bear little similarity to the dreams and aspirations to which we have given our lives. No longer can we be satisfied trying to do the North American Dream with a little Jesus overlay. Belatedly we have discovered that the self-seeking, materialistic aspirations of the Land of Evermore will never satisfy our deepest desire to find meaning in life. Obviously there is no place in God's dream for "doing what's best for myself first" since God is fashioning a new servant community that lives by the principle, "in honor preference one another."

And the Scripture is clear: we are not headed for a dis-embodied existence in the clouds. Even as Christ was raised from the dead we are going to be resurrected as whole persons, to be a part of God's new heaven and new earth. We will join millions of others from every tongue and tribe and culture going up to Mount Zion to the wedding feast of God to celebrate the Creator's great homecoming.

And there is no hint in the biblical story that God intends to erect a U.S. super-state to redeem the world. God's agenda transcends the limited ideological agendas of U.S. liberals and conservatives. God is creating a new transnational order in which all nations, including the United States, will be judged.

The creator God intends to make all things new. God's king-dom is both present and coming. Both now and not yet. And those who are finding a meaningful way of life are those who have joined the Creator in this adventure.

What Are God's Purposes for the Human Future?

Incredibly, the Creator God, stands at the threshold of history in making you and me to join in the drama of seeing God's world changed in same partial ways now in anticipation of Christ's return when all thing will be made new. I am con-vinced that the caring way we are going to find the meaningful way of life we all care for is to join the Lord of history in the venture of seeing God's world changed. Then and only then will we find another way up . . . a way of life that really counts.

And of course the only way we can join in this historical venture is to be very clear as to what the Creator's caring pur-poses are for God's people and God's world. As we reflect on the sweeping story of God, we need to ask: "What seems to be God's purpose for the human future?" The Creator God in-tends to create—

a new international community of celebration in which we will come home to Zion to reign with our Creator forever;

a new era of peace and Shalom in which the instruments of war are transformed into implements of peace;

a new order of justice in which there is no more oppression of the poor;

a new era of righteousness in which are corporate and individual sin will be put away and all evil ended;

a new world of compassion in which the blind see, the deaf hear—and everything partial is made whole;

a world in which the beauty and harmony of creation have been restored; even the wastelands will bloom.

a jubilant wedding feast on the mountain of God, where we will celebrate with sisters and brothers from every tongue, tribe, and culture.

Remember when Jesus stood up in his hometown at the beginning of his ministry and read out of Isaiah 61, "The Spirit of the Lord is upon me, because he annointed me to preach the Gospel to the poor. He sent me to proclaim release to the captives, and recovery of sight to the blind, to set free those who are down and to proclaim the favorable year of the Lord . . . (Luke 4:17-21 NASB). Again what it meant for Jesus to be the Messiah of God was to devote his life to working for the loving purposes of God.

In the first century you couldn't claim to be a follower of this Jesus simply by believing about God in your heart and going about life as usual. If you were to be a disciple of Jesus you too were expected to reorder your life around the other serving purposes of God.

If you too choose to follow this Jesus, it will require putting first things first. God's mission purposes before your economic aspirations . . . or anything else. If you do it will likely necessitate reordering your timestyle and lifestyle around a new set of purposes. For some it may even involve quitting jobs or relocating as it did for some of those first disciples.

But if you join millions of others who have proceeded us in this adventure you will not only find a new way up you will find a way of life truly that counts.

In the next chapter we will look at a handful of those in our past who chose to put first things first and you will see how God used their lives to make a difference in the world in which they lived and served.

FOR THOUGHT AND DISCUSSION

As you reflect on the story of God, ask yourself:

1. What are God's purposes to make a world new? How can we work for God's purposes now?
2. How does God's dream for human future differ from the dreams we discussed in chapter 2?
3. If you decided to put God's purposes first in your life how would it change the way you order your life? How would it change the direction of your life?

Vision of God

life linked to the purposes of God

life direction	linkages	consequences
God's story makes it clear that God has a dream for us and God's good creation. God's dream is not to transport us to the Land of Evermore, help us do what is "best for ourselves first," erect a super state for Jesus, or rescue us into a dis-embodied existence in the clouds. Our God intends to redeem us as a part of a recreated world in which the blind see, the deaf hear, and the lame dance with joy. Even as Jesus was a man for others working for the purposes of God . . . we are invited to be a people for others putting God's dream and God's loving purposes first in our lives as did those first disciples.	Those first believers set aside the self-involved aspirations of their culture to follow Jesus. They linked their lives to the purposes of God by extending God's love by word and deed into their world.	As a direct consequence of linking their lives to the purposes of God, those first Christians sensed that they were part of a venture that was quite literally changing their world. By the power of the Spirit they became known as those "who were tearing the world upside down." And our world has never been the same since those first Christians began spreading the good news beyond to the most remote parts of our earth.

Remembering Stories of Hope

Remembering! One of the marvelous gifts of human experience is remembering. When we look backward, we remember who we are and are becoming. We recall those tender moments with those we love, and we relish those carnival moments when we become children again. Even painful memories of loss somehow instruct us and become part of who we are.

This is true of our personal lives—and also of our collective past. For the road to more significant living begins not only with becoming more fully connected to God's story and God's purposes but also by remembering those who have gone before who have sought to live out that story. For as we saw in the last chapter, the vast drama of God didn't end in the book of Acts. Each succeeding generation has had its moment in the spotlights as the church age marches toward consummation.

Looking backward and seeing God's drama acted out in history reminds us of who we are and are called to be. Remembering our Christian past strengthens our resolve to live out the story of God with courage and compassion today. We are given heroes we can look up to. They show us a new way up.

There are thousands of such heroes. In this chapter, we will meet a handful. You will note that they are ordinary people . . . possessed by an extraordinary commitment to put God's purposes first. We will take a remembering journey into some compelling moments from our common past. *The purpose in this chapter is to help us find in the stories of those who have gone before the courage and commitment to follow Christ today, to place the purposes of God at the very center of our lives so that we too can find a way of life that truly counts . . . a new way up.*

Remembering Who We Are

When we rummage through the attics of our memories we often come up with strange items. For example, I remember traveling for World Concern to visit development projects in Bangladesh. Bud and Patti Bylsma, who were directing the work from Dacca, kindly put me up for the night. I had heard that the area had recently experienced the immigration of an awesome population of mosquitoes, some of which carried malaria. So, explaining that mosquitoes adored my body, I asked Bud and Patti if I could borrow some mosquito repellent.

Bud came up with a tiny dark-green bottle. He said it was the most effective mosquito repellent he had ever found, and he assured me the mosquitoes wouldn't even come into the same room with me if I used the stuff.

He told me to rub it thoroughly over all the exposed areas of my body and wished me a good night's rest. I followed his instructions. As I rubbed the goo over my arms, I noticed that it developed an interesting white frothy appearance. No matter. I used the whole bottle on my face, neck, arms, and legs.

After an exhausting day visiting fish ponds, agricultural projects, and rice paddies, I crashed in my hot, muggy room, looking forward to a good night's sleep. But no sooner had I turned out the light when I sensed I was not alone in the bed. A pricking pain in my leg convinced me I was right.

I dispatched the mosquito with one hand and turned the

light on with the other. Must have missed a spot! After sighting a couple more mosquitoes flying near the curtains, I did them in, turned out the light, and rolled over to go to sleep again. Then just as I was dozing off I was dive-bombed, submarined, and blitzkrieged all at the same time.

I spent the rest of the night in armed combat—attacking and being attacked. When morning came, the room was a disaster. Bedding everywhere. Blood spots all over the walls and ceiling where I had terminated my unwelcome intruders. My body was a mass of mosquito welts.

When Bud and Patti saw me dragging myself to the breakfast table, they sensed it had been an unusual evening. They were astonished as I told them of my nightlong foray.

I returned Bud's little green bottle and made some unkind remark about reporting the company to the Better Business Bureau. They were completely puzzled. But suddenly a broad smile broke across Bud's face. "Doggone, I completely forgot we used up all the mosquito repellent; I filled that little bottle with shampoo. You made yourself into a gigantic mosquito dessert!" He and Patti almost fell off their chairs laughing.

I was rude. I didn't join in. But as the years have passed I've been able to appreciate the humor in the situation a little more. Sometimes things appear funnier when you look back on them than they did at the time. A little distance sharpens perspective.

The Jews were uniquely a people of remembrance and a people of anticipation. They lived in remembrance of God's acts in their past and in anticipation of God's promises for the future. In fact, their entire sense of identity as a people was linked to remembering and looking forward.

Listen to the plaintive cry of Jewish exiles from Psalm 137.

> By the rivers of Babylon we sat down; there we wept when we remembered Zion. On the willows nearby we hung up our harps. Those who captured us told us to sing; they told us to entertain them: "Sing us a song about Zion." But how can we sing a song to the Lord in a foreign land? May I never be able to play the harp again if I forget you, Jerusalem!

Of course they didn't forget Jerusalem. And they did eventually return home to Jerusalem and Zion with incredible joy, dancing, and feasting. Their strength was in their memory—because they never forgot who they were. As a consequence they were able to return home.

If you and I are to come home to all God intends for us, then it is essential that we remember who we are, too. We must remember not only the stories of Jerusalem and Zion, but also the other exhilarating, life-directing stories of our Christian past. There are thousands of such stories whose remembrance can renew our lives and set right our rudders. Here we have time for only a few.

To help us remember, we will take some imaginative journeys back in time. The places we will visit are real, as are the people living there. The stories in which we will participate are based on accounts of actual happenings in those people's lives.

If our remembering works as I hope it will, we will glimpse the lives of Christians of other days. In the process, we may be reminded who we are and who we are called to be. And we will gain a fresh awareness of the secret that lives deep inside of us: we are destined to a better way of life—better not only for us but also for all those with whom we share this world. We are following in the lineage of a great company of servants and saints who have collaborated with God to change the world.

A Remembering Journey to a Roman Tribunal

To get underway, simply set your imagination free, buckle your seat belt, and prepare to move rapidly back in time to the third century A.D. Our remembering journey has begun.

Now look around. We have arrived. (Sorry. We have landed in a huge convoy behind a camel, and he is aromatic.) It's hard to see where we're going, but the rolling countryside around us is parched, the heat intense. There are children everywhere.

Look over that rise. The front of the caravan seems to be entering that walled city in the distance. Faint wisps of cloud streak the bright blue sky, the sun is reflecting off domed roofs, and the walls give off a soft, golden glow. A narrow column of smoke is rising from a clearing inside the walls. Look at the red poppies by the wall. The camel in front of us is absolutely loaded down with leeks, onions, grapes—and those must be olives.

As we make our way through the gates, the crowd heads for a large structure at the end of the road. My guess is that we have landed in a town somewhere in Palestine. On the veranda of the building stands a group of people in chains, waiting.

"In the name of the Emperor Maximinus, let the trials begin!" declares a Roman soldier. A portly, toga-clad gentleman seats himself at the table of judgment; we hear someone behind us whisper that he is Severus, the governor of the province.

As a young man in chains is brought forward, Severus asks, "What is your name?"

"My family name is Balsam, but I received the name of Peter in baptism."

Severus: "Of what family and country are you?"

Peter: "I am a Christian."

Severus: "What is your employment?"

Peter: "What employment can I have more honorable, or what better thing can I do in the world, than to be a Christian?"

Severus: "Do you know the imperial edicts?"

Peter: "I know the laws of God, the sovereign of the universe."

Severus: "Know that there is an edict of the most clement of emperors, commanding all to sacrifice to the gods or die."

Peter: "You will know one day that there is a law of the eternal King, proclaiming that everyone shall perish who offers sacrifice to devils. Which do you counsel me? To obey? Or be condemned to everlasting misery by the great King, the true God?"

Severus: "Since you ask my advice, it is that you obey the edict and sacrifice to the gods."

Peter: "I can never be prevailed upon to sacrifice to gods of wood and stone, as are those which you worship."

Severus: "I would have you know that it is in my power to avenge those affronts by putting you to death."

Peter: "I had no intention of affronting you. I only expressed what is written in the divine law."

During this exchange, the governor grows visibly frustrated.

His voice rises a little as he continues, "Have compassion on yourself. Sacrifice."

But Peter answers, "I am truly compassionate to myself, thus I ought not sacrifice."

The governor tries a different tack. "I want to be lenient; I shall allow you time to reflect, that you may save your life."

But again the young man replies, "This delay will be to no purpose, for I shall not alter my mind. Do now what you will do, and complete the work which the devil, your father, has begun. For I will never do what Jesus Christ forbids me."

The words enrage Severus, who orders that Peter be stretched on the rack. The crowd murmurs as soldiers suspend the young Christian on a wooden instrument nearby. Then the governor scoffs, "What say you now, Peter; do you begin to know what the rack is? Are you yet willing to sacrifice?"

Peter answers, "Tear me with hooks, and talk not of my sacrificing to your devils; I have already told you that I will sacrifice only to that God for whom I suffer."

Whereupon the governor commands Peter's torture to be intensified. But the young man, instead of crying out, sings verses from the Scriptures. "One thing I have asked of the Lord; this will I seek after: that I may dwell in the house of the Lord all the days of my life. I will take the chalice of salvation, and will call upon the name of the Lord."

The spectators, seeing Peter's blood run in streams, cry, "Obey the emperor. Sacrifice. Rescue yourself from torment!"

But Peter replies, "Do you call this torment? I feel no pain; but this I know, that if I be not faithful to my God, I must expect real pain, such as cannot be conceived."

The judge threatens, "Sacrifice, Peter Balsam, or be sorry."

Peter: "Neither will I sacrifice, nor shall I be sorry."

Severus: "I am on the point of pronouncing sentence."

Peter: "It is what I most earnestly desire."

And so Severus dictates Peter's sentence in this manner: "It is our order that Peter Balsam, for having refused to obey the edict of the invincible emperors, and obstinately defending the law of a crucified man, be himself nailed to a cross."

They lead Peter away, his head uplifted, to face the same death his Lord had known. . . .[1]

100 Live It Up!

Peter Balsam was just one of thousands of Christians asked in those early years to lay down their lives for their Lord. He was crucified over two hundred years after the crucifixion of the one whose story he so fully embraced.

A Remembering Journey to the Family of Hy

Ready for another trip? We're going to about A.D. 565 this time. I recommend you bring a coat; our remembering journey will take us north.

Here we are. Don't be alarmed. This cowhide and wicker boat is completely safe, and it sure beats following a camel!

I think those guys in the back of the boat want us to row, too; they are handing us round wooden paddles. Behind us is a rugged coastline banked with large cumulus clouds. We are surrounded by rough choppy seas. And we seem to be heading for that small island over there, though the irregular course of our boat makes it unclear where we are headed. (I'm sure our rowing has something to do with that.)

My best guess is that we are off the coast of Scotland somewhere. Notice it's considerably cooler than Palestine. The island we are slowly approaching couldn't be much more than three miles long. It's relatively flat except for that huge rock outcropping at the north end shaped like a loaf of bread. The entire island, including the sides of the outcropping, appears upholstered in a luxurious, shamrock-green velvet.

Remarkably, we have left the clouds behind. And this isle is framed in singular beauty against the expansive cloudless blue sky. One can sense something special about the place.

Look out! We almost hit those rocks. Now we see a small collection of stick-and-stone wattle huts to the right to the primitive harbor where we appear to be heading. They have a welcoming party to greet us. They appear to be wearing coarse, brown, woven robes.

The welcome couldn't be warmer. Several of them have run into the cold surf and almost capsized the boats getting us ashore. We are embraced by these rough-clad greeters.

They usher us to their largest dwelling, a basic round structure of mud and thatch. Marvelous aromas greet us as we enter. As our eyes become accustomed to the seal-oil light, we see a rough wooden table laden with food—joints of mutton, roasted fish, wild berries, pitchers of milk, barley loaves, and fresh butter. They have been expecting us, though they don't understand who we are. They treat us as royalty. I think they call themselves the family of Hy.

After dinner they invite us to worship. To our amazement, we don't go to a chapel or some type of crude sanctuary; we climb the huge rock outcropping we had seen from the boat. At the top we have a spectacular view of the Scottish coastline on one side and the Atlantic Ocean on the other. In this outdoor setting, we sense that these people's spirituality is inseparably related to creation itself.

Columba, head of this unusual family, gestures for us from a large circle. He leads us in a simple liturgy of chanting, reading, and song. The songs are particularly moving; the family sings with such joy they almost break into dancing. Then, as the sun begins to set over the isle of Iona, Columba raises his large hands; all heads bow. As he prays passionately in his rhythmic Gaelic dialect, we sense this is a special place of God's favor.

Morning comes early, and after a brief breakfast of barley cakes and milk, Columba and two other brothers escort us back to the harbor and join us in the cowhide boat. We cross the choppy water to the mainland, then trudge over the rough terrain until we come to a village of Picts.

With one of the brothers translating for him, Columba preaches the gospel to the villagers. Immediately an entire family believes, and he baptizes them in a stream nearby. Shortly afterward we say good-bye, and our small party journeys on.

Several days later, while staying in a village miles up the coast, we receive a report that the son of the household which had been converted was seized by a severe illness and died suddenly. When the boy became ill, magicians in the community began to taunt the boy's parents and belittle the Christian God as too weak to intervene. When Columba hears what has happened, he says we must return.

We arrive just as the parents are performing the funeral

rites. Columba interrupts the service and asks to be taken to the
boy's dead body. He enters the dwelling alone, tears streaming
down his face. From where we are standing outside, we can
hear him say, "In the name of the Lord Jesus Christ, be restored
to life and stand up." A few minutes later he reappears, leading
the child by the hand. The boy's parents cry out and run to embrace their son. A shout arises from the people.

Mourning is turned into rejoicing—the God of the Christians is glorified. Unfortunately, we aren't able to stay around to
watch Columba deal with the magician. . . .[2]

Columba and his followers not only carried the good news
of the story from Iona to Scotland but to England and much of
Europe. This aggressive Celtic Christianity brought the joy and
vitality of God's story wherever it went, because the Celts
placed God's purposes first in their lives and community.

A Remembering Journey to the Bishop's Palace in Arezzo

Our next remembering journey takes us south and six
centuries forward. The year is 1289. The climate is warmer.

We find ourselves seated in the splendor of a palace somewhere in Italy. Above us soar vaulted ceilings. Elegant furnishings announce that we are in a place of wealth and power.

Look, the man coming in that large door—he's dressed like a
bishop. As he settles his frame in a larger chair, a visitor is announced: Margaret of Cortona. As she enters the chamber, the
contrast between the two people is striking; her clothing is as
simple as the bishop's costume is extravagant. But it is clear that
Bishop William of Arezzo takes Margaret of Cortona seriously.

She explains that she comes as an emissary from God. She
has received a divine warning that the bishop should cease conflict with other powerful men in his diocese and thus avert war.

The bishop listens respectfully. But he shakes his head heavily as she leaves. What she said was not what he wanted to hear.

Who is this Margaret who speaks so confidently to a bishop?
We walk around the palace until we find a clerk painstakingly
transcribing a document. He tells us that three years ago the

bishop granted Margaret a charge enabling her to work for the sick and the poor on a permanent basis. And he doesn't need much encouragement to lay down his pen and tell us what he has heard about this remarkable woman's background.

It seems Margaret was not always a woman who walked closely with God and cared for others. A dashing young man from Montepulciano induced Margaret to run away with him, promising to marry her. But he never did.

Margaret lived with him as his mistress and bore one son. Then one day the young man failed to return from touring his estates, and his dog led Margaret to the shallow grave where his murdered master had been buried.

The tragic event shattered Margaret's world and confronted her with the judgment of God. She turned her life back to the Creator, and two Franciscan priests became her fathers in Christ. But that was only the beginning of the struggle.

For the next three years, Margaret went through turbulent battles with temptations and depression. On one of these occasions she said, "Father, do not ask me to come to terms with this body of mine, for I cannot afford it. Between me and my body there must needs be a struggle till death."

Initially Margaret earned a living by nursing the rich women in the city. But eventually she gave up this work to have more time for prayer and the care of the poor. She began to subsist on handouts. Any unbroken food she got she gave to the poor.

After her son went to school in Arezzo, one of Margaret's deepest prayers was answered; she was invited to become a member of the third order of Franciscans. Now her prayer life soared. From time to time she even received prophetic insights from God, such as the one she just delivered to Bishop William.

At this point, however, the clerk shakes his head—just as the bishop did. Margaret has gained respect for her good works, he tells us, but perhaps she is going too far. She is becoming controversial; some have even begun to question her conversion.

We thank the clerk and take our leave of the palace, but we linger awhile in town. We talk to many who are convinced Margaret is a woman of God. Others are skeptical. We learn that the town is astir because the bishop is preparing for war. . . .

If we had stayed a little longer, we would have heard the news that the bishop had been killed in battle—ten days after Margaret delivered her message. And we would have seen Margaret's ministry continue to grow. For God led Margaret into a public ministry of evangelism, reconciliation, and healing that not only confirmed what God had done in her life, but demonstrated how God can use an ordinary person in extraordinary ways. Through the ministry of this single mother, God called wrongdoers to repentance, reconciled those alienated from one another, attacked public vice, healed the sick, and preached good news to the poor.

Hardened sinners flocked to Cortona from Spain, France, and other parts of Italy to hear Margaret preach. Not only did countless numbers come to faith in Christ, but even the character of the town of Cortona changed as they began to acknowledge the reign of God in their midst.

As Margaret of Cortona placed the purposes of God at the center of her life, she found her role in God's story. And she found a new way up.[3]

A Remembering Journey to a Bible Study in Belgium

We're headed north again, this time about three hundred years into the future. You can almost sense the landscape changing as we travel into the night.

I'm not sure where we've landed this time; it's too dark to see. But it's quite warm; it feels like springtime. There are some flickering lights over to the right. Let's go over there. Our eyes gradually adjust to the darkness as we approach an old mill. Then the door opens. People are leaving, extinguishing their lamps to walk through the night. Let's follow that family headed for town from what appears to be a clandestine Bible study.

Birds begin to call to one another from darkly sculptured oak trees as Maeyken Wens and her husband, Matthews, both of whom were leading Bible studies, hurry home with their children. No sooner do they get to their tiny home in an ancient building in Antwerp than Matthews has to go to work. He hides his Bible under the bed, grabs a crust of bread and his mason's tools, kisses Maeyken warmly, and leaves.

Maeyken plays with their three-year-old, Hans—chasing him, catching him, hugging him, and making him laugh uproariously. Fifteen-year-old Adriean and his sister fix themselves and us some breakfast of bread and cheese. Maeyken finally calms her chunky Hans, gives him some milk and bread, and puts him to bed in an old basket.

She picks up her Bible and hides it under her cloak, hugs her two older children, and heads for the door. Outside she looks cautiously both ways, then proceeds north up the narrow cobblestone roadway. We follow a short distance behind her.

Look. Another woman with a bulge under her stole is joining Maeyken. I can't believe it. Apparently it's Bible study time again—but they've been up all night studying the Bible. I don't know how Maeyken does it; she has remarkable energy.

Two more people join the parade; they seem to be headed for that stop at the next corner. A group gathers in front, welcoming Maeyken and the others as they arrive.

Oh no! Soldiers. They swoop down from nowhere and surround the entire group. Where are they taking our friends? Let's try to keep them in sight.

They seem to be heading for that huge castle. They are dragging the women inside and taking away their Bibles.

Anabaptists. That's who these people are. They have the unique distinction of being persecuted by both Protestants and Catholics.

Let's wait here out of sight. The word must have reached the community; here comes Maeyken's family. Matthews is holding Betteken's hand, and Adriean is carrying Hans. They are obviously troubled, and Matthews looks ill. He must be risking his own life to visit his wife.

After a long delay, the family finally receives permission to visit Maeyken in the Steen prison. We follow them in. She is elated to see her small family. She reaches her slender fingers through the lattice of the cell door to touch each of her three children. Hans sticks his arm through for his mother's kiss.

There seems to be no fear in Maeyken's voice; she is obviously encouraging her husband and other children to maintain their faith whatever happens. We are ushered out of that dark, smelly hole as the prison suddenly becomes alive with the powerful music of women's voices singing a hymn of praise.

Now we jump ahead a bit. Maeyken's family has kept hoping and praying for the release of their mother and her friends, but nothing has happened. Then they learn that Maeyken has been sentenced to death because she will not recant her personal faith in Jesus Christ.

Matthews is overcome by grief; he cannot bring himself to attend his wife's execution. But young Adriean feels he must go. Leaving his sister and father behind, he takes Hans by the hand, and they slowly make their way to Antwerp's central square.

Look. They are already putting the stakes in the ground. A huge throng is forming. Adriean and Hans have no sooner found a place to sit than the jailers bring in five prisoners, including Maeyken. She walks resolutely toward the stake, her face beaming, but she says nothing. The jailers have put a tongue screw through her tongue so that she cannot speak nor tell the crowd of her faith. As she is tied to the stake and wood is heaped up around, Adriean is overwhelmed by the horror of what is happening. He crumples to the ground and blacks out.

Some time later, Adriean regains consciousness and looks around. The square is almost completely empty. Hans stands there quietly watching him. He looks at the stake and sees nothing but a pile of smoldering ashes. His mother is gone. He weeps uncontrollably while Hans tries to console him. Finally he picks up a stick and digs through the ashes. All he can find is the iron tongue screw, which he wraps in a handkerchief to remember his mother's courage.

When Adriean gets back home, he finds a letter his mother had written to him.

> O my son, though I am taken from you here, strive from your youth to fear God, and you shall have your mother again up yonder in the New Jerusalem, where parting will be no more. My dear son, I hope to go before you; follow me in this way as much as you value your soul, for besides this there can be no other way to salvation. So I will now commend you to the Lord;

may he keep you. I trust the Lord that he will do it, if you seek Him. Love one another all the days of your life, take Hansken on your arm now and then for me. And if your father should be taken from you, care for one another. The Lord keep you one and all. My dear children, kiss one another once for me, for remembrance. Adieu, my dear children, all of you. . . .[4]

Anabaptists such as the Wenses were just one example of Christians who suffered for their beliefs during the turbulent period called the Reformation (1517-1648). By the end of this time, the Christian world had been turned upside down, and Europe had been split in half between Catholics and Protestants—not to mention dissenting groups of Protestants.

On a recent trip to Europe, I found the church in which my grandfather's grandfather was married in 1780. The church, constructed in 1730, is actually two churches—one Catholic and one Protestant, with a common roof and a common bell tower. In my mind, this church symbolizes what happened to Christendom as a result of the Reformation. The church was no longer monolithic and unified, but divided in many different expressions of faith. Yet the story of God remains one story.

Although the Reformation did bring turmoil, suffering, and division to the church, it also brought renewal and reform. And of course the spirit of reform and renewal didn't end in the seventeenth century. Over the years groups such as Moravians, Methodists, and many others attempted to give fresh expression to the faith of their fathers and mothers by placing God's living purposes first in their lives.

A Remembering Journey to Newgate Prison

Now we will take still another journey forward in time. This has to be the industrial age! All around us is noise and bustle, and that building over there looks like a foundry.

Where are we? From the architecture and the clothes people are wearing, I would guess in England—London, probably—in the early 1800s.

It *is* London—that forbidding compound over there has a sign that identifies it as the infamous Newgate Prison. Look, there's a solitary young woman walking up to the massive prison gates. She doesn't look as if she belongs here; she's well-dressed and carrying a Bible. She's asking for an audience with the prison governor. What could she have to say to him?

When the governor appears, the woman introduces herself as Elizabeth Fry. Then she speaks in gentle Quaker accents. "Sir, if thee kindly allows me to pray with the women, I will go inside." (To tell the truth, after our last adventure, I'm inclined to avoid prisons. But let's follow her anyway.)

The smell hits us first. Then we see them—300 women prisoners and their children, blinking back at us. Dressed in rags, they are thin and sickly looking from trying to exist in four basement rooms without beds or sanitation. A filthy old woman with crazed eyes yells and snatches at our clothing as we pass.

Elizabeth Fry stands before us overcome at what she has discovered hidden in the brutal bowels of Newgate. She says a feeble prayer as the women and children stare at their unlikely visitor. Then she escapes back into the streets.

Back out in the bright light and fresh air, Elizabeth hurries away, dabbing at her eyes. But then she walks more slowly and even turns her head for another look at the forbidding walls. It is clear that something—or someone—is calling her back. . . .

Elizabeth Fry accepted God's challenge to go back to Newgate Prison. Though a busy wife and mother, she joined with other Quakers in 1816 to found the Association for the Improvement of Female Prisoners in Newgate. And of course she undertook personal risk to work directly with the women prisoners.

The initial goals were modest—to try to clean up the abominable living conditions and provide the women with clothing, employment, and instruction. Elizabeth herself personally instituted a Bible study program to help these women understand that God's love is extended to everyone regardless of class station. Many women prisoners were powerfully moved as she read the Scriptures, and many came to faith in Jesus Christ.

Elizabeth Fry's faithfulness to God's call spawned a sweeping movement of prison reform that would touch lives in institutions in Europe, Australia, and America. By ordering her life around the purposes of God, Elizabeth was used of God to impact the lives of women on three continents.

As Elizabeth's ministry of prison reform blossomed, her husband's business failed, and they had to learn to live much more modestly. But she found she was more comfortable with a simpler way of life, because she believed luxurious living was a serious threat to the spirit.

On her deathbed, Elizabeth Fry reflected on the drama of God in which she had played a part. "I can say one thing—since my heart was touched . . . I believe I never have awakened from sleep, in sickness or in health, by day or night, without my first waking thought being how best I might serve my Lord."[5]

A Remembering Journey to Wheaton College

Our final journey takes us a littler farther into the future and across the Atlantic Ocean. The same winds of the Spirit that inspired Elizabeth Fry, William Wilberforce, and John Wesley have brought a Great Awakening on this continent, stirred by the preaching of Charles Finney. People are coming to radical faith in Jesus Christ and are committing themselves to change the world of which they are a part. Slavery, alcohol, and war are all under attack by this generation of born-again Christians.

Let's take one last trip to an American city in the 1800s. It is a cold, blustery October day. From the layout of this city I would guess we have landed in Chicago. But I must be wrong; this looks like a war zone. Scarcely a building is left standing. Smoldering ruins everywhere. People huddle together trying to keep warm. Families cook over campfires on the sidewalks.

And the street scene looks like a reenactment of the Exodus. Wagons bulging with belongings. Children perched perilously on top. Masses of people with bundles on their backs.

All the wagons, donkey carts, and people are going in one direction—out of town, away from this chaos. But wait! There's a solitary wagon with a lanky driver doing his best to come *into* town. People seem oblivious to his efforts, but somehow his persistence is paying off. He's getting through.

Some of the families cooking over the campfires spot him

and start running toward the wagon. The driver pulls his wagon into a clearing and immediately starts passing out food and milk to the homeless. They almost turn his wagon upside down as he passes out the last parcel.

The year is 1871. The tragedy is the great Chicago fire. The determined driver is Jonathan Blanchard, president of Wheaton College—a man whose entire life has been committed to God and a determination to make a difference.

This is a man who once declared, "Every true minister of Christ is a universal reformer, whose business it is, so far as is possible, to reform all evils which press on human concerns." Blanchard fully realized that one "cannot construct a perfect society out of imperfect men," but he argued that "every reformer needs a perfect state of society ever in his eye, as a pattern to work by, so as far as the nature of his materials will admit."[6] Little did Jonathan Blanchard realize, when he said this, how his vision for the kingdom of God would impact the direction of his own life, let alone the lives of countless others.

Again and again Blanchard's faith propelled him into a life of reform because he placed God's purposes first. He became active in the abolitionist movement, eloquent in advocacy of the poor, firm in opposition to intemperance of war "and whatever else shall clearly appear to contravene the kingdom and the coming of our Lord Jesus Christ."[7]

In 1860 Jonathan Blanchard accepted the invitation to be president of Wheaton College. He later said, "I came to Wheaton in 1860, still seeking 'a perfect state of society' and a college 'for Christ and His kingdom.' "[8]

Blanchard understood that we are called to be a part of God's work in establishing his reign in history. In fact, he once defined the kingdom of God as "Christ ruling in and over rational creatures who are obeying him freely and from choice, under no constraint but love."[9]

Back to the Present—and the Future

Welcome back to the present. We have at least as many needs, challenges, and opportunities in our world as anything

Peter Balsam, Columba, Margaret of Cortona, Maeyken Wens, Elizabeth Fry, or Jonathan Blanchard faced in theirs. But do we have their vision for the kingdom of God? Are we taking God's story and purposes for the future as seriously as they did? What would happen if we, like they, chose to put God's purposes first?

As we return from our remembering journey, our minds are flooded with images and memories of those who had the courage to place God's vision first in their lives. Obviously there is much that can nurture and challenge us as we remember the stories of our Christian past. We are a part of a historic movement that the Creator God is using to change the world. Where could a person possibly find a more meaningful way of life than as part of this ongoing drama of God? Interested? Then the next chapter will be your opportunity to come onstage and chose to put God's purposes first in your life.

FOR THOUGHT AND DISCUSSION

1. What specific choices did people in this chapter make to place God's purposes first in their lives?
2. How did their commitment alter the direction of their lives and influence their world?
3. In what ways have these stories challenged you more fully to commit your life to working for the purposes of God . . . to finding a new way up?

life directions	linkages	consequences
God's story is ongoing, and God's vision has captured the imaginations and commitment of people in all generations. As Christians through the centuries have sought to put God's purposes first, they have become a part of the unfolding vision of God's loving intentions to make all things new.	Our Christian past is filled with the stories of tens of thousands who have chosen to link their lives to the purposes of God. Their stories challenge us to follow their example—and invite us to join them in placing God's purposes first.	Our forebears not only discovered life with meaning; by God's Spirit, their lives also made a difference! They dramatically changed the landscape of our common past as a foretaste of all God plans to do in our promised future. As we follow their example, God will use our lives too making a difference in a needy world.

Choosing a Life That Counts

hoosing! One of the exciting and risky gifts of our humanity is choice. God gave that gift to our first parents. And they chose to turn their backs on their Creator and all God intended for their lives. The history of the children of Israel is a history of rebellious people who chronically struggled with choosing whether to serve God or go their own way.

Christ came inviting people to choose to set aside their lesser dreams and join him in committing their lives to God. And over the centuries, as we have seen, many chose to follow Christ and put first things first; and their lives made a difference.

Every day countless choices confront us. But none is more important than the decision to follow this Christ and put God's purposes at the center of our lives, families, and congregations.

Remarkably, many have accepted Christ into their hearts but have never embraced Christ's vision for a world made new. How can we ever be satisfied with the self-seeking aspirations of the North American dream once we understand that God invites us to be a part of another vision that is destined to change a world?

The purpose of this chapter is to persuade you not only to commit your life to God but to placing the purposes of God at the absolute center of your life . . . to find a new way up like those who have gone before us.

A Word from Tony

When I think of stories, I'm always reminded of Tony Campolo—he's full of stories. One thing I dread worse than walking barefoot on broken bottle-glass is following Tony Campolo in a speaking situation. The reason is that he bursts at the seams with stories, humorous anecdotes, and one-liners.

Once while working with Tony at a church conference in the Midwest, I confessed my dread to him. I told him I thought he was the evangelical answer to Don Rickles—with substance, minus the insults. I explained that I hated following him because I lack his marvelous anecdotes.

His sympathetic response was immediate, "I will give you a story."

I asked hesitatingly, "Is it true?"

"Of course it's true," he replied.

Tony explained that he was flying from his home in Philadelphia to be keynote speaker at a youth conference. Busily working on his notes on the plane, he suddenly found he was having difficulty breathing. A horrendous odor filled the cabin. It smelled as if the plane was on fire.

Tony stood up and looked around to see what was happening. There on the other side of the aisle in the nonsmoking section was a very large man. His even larger cigar was putting out clouds of putrid blue cigar smoke.

Tony said, "Being the brave guy that I am, I immediately called the flight attendant and asked her to talk to this joker."

The attendant gave the man the standard spiel, requesting that he go to the back of the plane if he wanted to smoke and reminding him cigar smoking was allowed nowhere on the plane.

The portly man didn't respond; he just rudely blew cigar

smoke in the attendant's face. She walked off in a huff.

Tony decided not to make an issue of it. He simply took a deep breath, tried to hold it until they landed, and went back to preparing his address. Fifteen minutes later, there came another flight attendant rushing down the aisle with a tray full of hot drinks. She had not talked to the first attendant and had no idea what had happened.

Just as she reached the point in the plane at which the confrontation had taken place, the plane hit an air pocket and dropped fifty feet. The tray of hot drinks went up in the air and came right down on the rude man, dousing his cigar. He jumped up screaming.

The stewardess fell backwards and landed right in Tony's lap. He was instantly ready with a one-liner: "And people say there's no God."

The point of this chapter—and this book—is that there *is* a God—and that God has a plan not only for our lives, but for God's world. If we want to discover how to live significant, satisfying lives that make a difference, it isn't enough simply to live out the stories and aspirations with which we were raised. It isn't enough simply to try to live up to the expectations of family, community, and church with a little faith worked in around the edges. We must, like those who have gone before us, make the conscious choice to embrace God's dream as our dream and God's purposes as our purposes. We are invited to a new way up by putting first things first.

A Crisis of Caring

We are facing a disturbing double crisis as we race toward the twenty-first century. Human suffering and need are escalating dramatically within both our global and national communities. At the same time the ability of the Western church to respond to these escalating needs is actually declining.

Globally the gap between the planetary rich and the planetary poor is increasing at a rapid rate. The population of many countries is growing faster than ability to feed and sustain the new arrivals. One doesn't have to be a demographer to realize this is going to mean increasing hunger and famine and starvation for millions. Add to that millions of children that will be orphaned by the global AIDS epidemic. Decaying cities, growing tribalism, ethnic conflict, and violence will wreak havoc.

Many Christians are unaware that we are going backward, not forward in global evangelization. Population growth is not only increasing the misery index, it is outstripping our efforts to share the good news. By the year 2,000, the percentage of people claiming to be Christian will have dropped from current levels.

In the United States we are not only experiencing a widening gap between rich and poor but between those who are older and younger. The new U.S. poor are children. One child in five in our country is born into poverty and the trend is worsening. Twenty-three to twenty-five million Americans can't read and write; many of them are young people. In the 1980s some Christian leaders told us the only issue that mattered was abortion. In the 1990s we need a rebirth of compassion for the kids that made it as well as the kids that didn't.

Add to that growing numbers of AIDS victims, millions destroying their lives with alcohol and drugs, the increase in elder abuse, growing racism, and the increasing violence in our homes and communities.

We are not doing a good job of evangelism at home either. With each new generation fewer and fewer of our young choose to be part of any Christian church.

As we rush toward the next century, it should be painfully clear that business as usual will not begin to address the escalating physical and spiritual needs filling our world. The only way we can respond to these mounting human challenges is for all Christians to fundamentally reorder our lives so we have more time and money to invest in advancing God's purposes.

But tragically just the opposite is happening. The North American dream is demanding more and more people's time and money and robbing it from God's kingdom. The average giving of the American Christians is 2.8 percent a year. And an infinitesimally small part of that amount is invested in addressing the needs of the poor or in evangelizing the unreached.

As I work with Christians all over the United States and Canada, I am deeply concerned at how few have time to be directly involved every week in working with abused children, evangelizing young couples, or caring for neglected seniors. In most churches I work with I find fewer than 20 percent who have even two hours a week to minister with those beyond the doors of home and church.

We seem content with a kind of surrogate servanthood— paying others to care and serve in our stead. This minimal response is tragically inadequate to address the escalating challenges to tomorrow's world.

Rarely do I find churches that either call people out of their busy, disengaged lives or help them reorder their lives so they have time and resources to invest in advancing the purposes of God. Hopefully this book can sound something of a wake-up call.

As we look toward the future of the church, all Western countries, including the United States, are likely to experience a continuing decline in the number of Christian young who choose to be a part of the church. With those under thirty entering a stagnant economy, they are having to work longer for less. As a consequence those young people who decide to stay in the church are likely to have significantly less discretionary time and money than their parents' generation to advance the work of God's kingdom. It is my reluctant forecast that they will not begin to support the church and its mission even at the modest level of today's church as we enter a new century.

Therefore, as the needs of our world continue to increase, our capacity in the Western church to respond will likely continue to decline. Unless we put first things first. We can, if we choose, turn this tragic trend around.

Decision Number One

Decision number one for those of us who have chosen to follow Jesus Christ is to choose, as Christ did, to place God's purpose first in our lives. As Jesus was a man for others, so are we called to be a people for others. To respond to the escalating needs of our world we will all need to reorder our lives around a renewed sense of Christian vocation.

Essential for us in choosing to put first things first is the need to clarify what Christian vocation is and isn't. We need to define the specifics of putting God first.

Two-Track Myth of Christian Vocation

The reason so many Christians are investing so little time and money in the advance of God's new order is that many subscribe to a two-track view of Christian commitment and vocation. On one track, for instance, are missionaries who go to Africa and give 150 percent of their lives for the gospel. On the other track are the rest of us, who stay home, pursue the American dream with a vengeance, show up at church, give of our leftovers and offer "a little word on the job for Jesus."

This two-track approach to Christian vocation is neither biblical nor will it enable us to respond to the challenges of tomorrow's world. The Scripture is unequivocal on this point. There is no double standard in the gospel. The Scripture calls all Christians to put first things first. All Christians are to be "missionaries" totally committed to the advance of God's kingdom.

The Myth "That Anything You Do Is Your Vocation"

Another fictional view of vocation is that whatever we do occupationally is automatically our Christian vocation. Virtually every Christian book I have read on career planning chronically confuses what we have to do to support ourselves economically with our Christian vocation. They aren't necessarily the same.

I agree with Martin Luther that "all we do should be done to the glory of God." But where does one find biblical support for the notion that one's job is automatically one's Christian vocation? Didn't a number of those first disciples quit their jobs to join Christ in working for the same vocational call that directed his life? Is it possible we Westerners have been seduced into giving too much of ourselves to economic occupations?

Of course we have a responsibility to support ourselves and

provide for our families. But don't we also have a responsibility, as disciples, to intentionally invest part of our lives in sharing God's love beyond the doors of our homes and churches?

As we read those stirring stories in the Gospels and the book of Acts, it is clear that those first believers had a very different view of vocation than we hold today. In the first century, you couldn't claim to be a follower of Jesus if you weren't doing the same thing he was—devoting your life to working for the purposes of God. Ministry wasn't optional for the early Christians as it typically is for Christians today. Vocation came first.

In the first century the bleachers were empty. All believers were down on the field actively making a difference in their world. And by the power of God's Spirit, they were known as the ones who turned the world upside down. The advance of God's kingdom, not of career, was at center.

Listen again to Christ's call to those first disciples:

> I tell you, do not worry about your life, what you will eat or drink; or about your body, what you will wear. Is not life more important than food, and the body more important than clothes? . . . For the pagans run after all these things, and your heavenly Father knows that you need them. But seek first his kingdom and his righteousness, and all these things will be given to you as well." (Matt. 6:25, 32-33, NIV)

Jesus couldn't be clearer. If we choose to follow him, we too must place advancing his kingdom before our personal aspirations. Let me offer a Christian definition of vocation and some contemporary examples of what it looks like today to put first things first.

Walter Brueggemann offers a fine definition of Christian vocation, which, he suggests, "is finding a purpose for being that is related to the purposes of God."[1]

Finding a Purpose for Being Through Our Occupations

Let me share the stories of a few people who have discovered through their occupations their purpose for "being in the world."

Al felt God had called him into getting a degree in engineering. The first job Al was offered was a high-paying position with good perks and benefits helping design cruise missiles for an aeronautics firm. Al turned down the job. Though he wasn't a pacifist, for him designing cruise missiles was counter-kingdom.

After searching for several months, he took a job redesigning cardiology technology. He felt this choice was a little closer to his sense of call.

Then one day, out of the blue, one of Al's friends invited him to visit an Easter Seal home for children with cerebral palsy. Now it all came into focus for Al. He went back to graduate school to learn how to use advance engineering design and computer systems to help children with cerebral palsy move and communicate for the kingdom of God.

Get the picture? Virtually any training, experience, or profession can, with a little creativity, be modified to promote the purposes of God's kingdom.

Tom Wilson, a strapping man in his early forties, had spent his entire adult life working in the building trades in Aberdeen, Scotland. He enjoyed his life and family. But since the kids were grown, he found himself looking for something more.

Sunday night at church, a missionary from Nepal shared slides and mentioned, in passing, the inability of United Mission to Nepal to find anyone to supervise the construction of a hospital in one of the poorest parts of Katmandu. Tom talked to his wife, Natalie. They flew to Nepal in three months.

Two years later, I met Tom and Natalie in Katmandu. The hospital was half-built, Tom was having the time of his life. He said, "Last week the Nepali pastor actually asked me to preach next Sunday." Tom said he responded, "Aye, pastor, you're getting pretty near the bottom of the barrel when you're asking the likes of me to preach the good news."

But Tom was the good news, not only because he was sharing his rich construction knowledge but because the Nepali workers genuinely loved him. Tom had found a way of life that made a difference . . . a new way up.

Tony Campolo was instrumental in enabling Eastern College to introduce an MBA unique in the United States. It prepares young men and women to be business entrepreneurs who start small businesses among the poor and marginalized in the United States and the world.

But most of the Christian colleges I visit are doing more to prepare students to fit into the world than to change it. Rarely do I find career planning services in these schools that help young people imagine creative ways to use their vocational training intentionally to advance God's purposes.

Finding a Purpose for Being Through Our Discretionary Time

Now if we can't find ways to advance God's purposes through our working hours, then we need to find a way through our discretionary time. I find most people, with a little creativity, can find one evening a week to put first things first.

One challenging group is InterVarsity in southern California, which works with college students at various California universities. InterVarsity calls the students to a "rad" brand of Christian discipleship that includes Bible study, community support groups, lifestyle change, and freeing up discretionary time every week to work for the purposes of God.

Staff not only trains students to do in-depth Bible studies but challenges them to apply the biblical principals to their lives. This has resulted in numbers of students living in shared households where they not only support one another but simplify their lifestyles and share resources to release their time to minister with those in need. Despite their demanding academic loads and part-time work, they set aside time every week not only to reach out and share God's love on their campuses but also to be directly involved in meeting urgent urban needs in their communities.

InterVarsity leadership challenges graduating seniors to invest more than an evening a week working for the purposes of God. They challenge the students to give God the first four to five years out of college to work with the homeless and poor on the streets of Los Angeles. Thank God many are becoming part of this "after-varsity" movement and making a difference.

Most of us could, like these college students, find an evening a week for God. Even families could learn to be families for others, spending one evening a week putting God first.

Once while speaking at a Presbyterian church in the Seattle area, I asked, "What is it that bonds U.S. Christian families together? What do we do together more than anything else?"

That's right. Sit-Com television, Big Mac hamburgers, and trips to the mall. I asserted what bonds North American Christian families more than anything else (just like non-Christian families) is what we consume together.

I told that congregation that I have never seen a church that facilitates Christian families having their lives bonded in service to others instead of consumerism. I have never found a church that enables parents and their kids to do ministry together to those in the community. This is a major blind spot.

I returned to that Presbyterian church a few weeks later. The church hadn't changed. But a woman told me, "I'm doing it."

"What are you doing?" I asked.

"Because of what you said, I've started spending one morning a week working with senior citizens who are bedfast, who are likely to lose their homes if someone doesn't help them with their chores. I go to these three homes every Wednesday morning and I take my two preschoolers with me. They don't watch mom work; they scrub the floor alongside me!"

What kind of kids would be raised if instead of eighteen years of indulgent living in the suburbs our Christian young did ministry every week with their parents? For all the Christian books and radio broadcasts about the family, isn't it past time for Christian families to put first things first—"Sight to the blind, release to the captives, and good news to the poor"?

Finding a Way Up Through Reordered Lives

Some Christians have quit their jobs and found ways to use those choice working hours for God. Others have found opportunities during discretionary time to make a difference. Still others creatively reordered their entire lives.

For example, a doctor I met in Denver sold half of his medical practice. He supports his family comfortably working twenty hours a week (of course some occupations pay too little to make this feasible). He is using the other twenty hours to start an inner-city health clinic for the poor.

Yet another version of what I call whole life stewardship was initiated by six graduates from Westmont College. They felt God was calling them to spend their lives with the young and poor in Oakland, California. Not surprisingly, no one was willing to give money for their ministry.

They moved to Oakland anyway. By renting and sharing an old house together they got by on $350 per person per month for rent, food, and utilities. As a consequence of their cooperative living situation, they found they could support themselves on half-time tent-making jobs.

Then the Westmont Six went to First Baptist Church in downtown Oakland and asked if they could open the gymnasium that had been locked up for years. Church leaders gave them the green light. The first night they opened the gym they immediately had forty to sixty inner city kids in off the streets playing basketball and receiving relational evangelism.

Discovering the Joy of Giving Life Away

The people I know who are having the best time, who have really found a way to live it up, are people who have learned the sheer joy of giving life away. My wife, Christine, a physician, said she has never known greater joy than seeing the way simple cleft palate surgery can transform a life.

She told me about meeting Lynette when the Mercy Ship *Anastasis,* which she was serving, stopped in Togo. Lynette, twenty-three, was hideously disfigured by a cleft lip that left a gaping hole in the side of her face. This was assumed in her tribe to be an evil curse; babies born with a cleft palate were normally put to death. Lynette had been rescued by her Christian grandparents, but had grown up ostracized by her village.

After the surgery, Lynette would sit by the house staring unbelievably at her "normal" face. After a few days a radiant smile broke across her face when she finally realized what had hap-

124   *Live It Up!*

pened. The following week she was fully reconciled to her family for the first time since birth. And she was enthusiastically welcomed home to her village as well.

Can you imagine anything more satisfying than playing a small part in seeing Lynette's life transformed? Well, you don't have to be a doctor in Togo to make a difference. There are kids in your own community who have been abandoned by their families for all kinds of reasons . . . who need to be touched by the love of God. There are seniors who are neglected and young people abusing drugs. The fields are indeed "white unto harvest but the laborers are few."

Choosing to Put First Things First

God participates in every part of our stories . . . in celebration and in suffering. But to participate in God's story, we must choose to put God's purposes before our own. And many of us struggle with that choice because we have been raised on a kind of compartmentalized discipleship.

But Scripture shows that God not only wants to change our hearts and heal our hang-ups but also to transform our life direction from upward mobility to outward ministry. If thousands of U.S., Canadian, and Western Christians decided to put first things first we would be amazed at what God could do through our mustard seeds. I am confident we would see a dramatic increase in the investment of our time and money to address the escalating challenges of tomorrow's world.

Putting First Things First . . . . A Guide to Finding Your Place in the Drama of God

Once we have made the choice to put first things first, how will we know our roll in the drama of God? How can we discover what our ministry should be, regardless of whether we are involved four, twenty, or forty hours a week?

Lily Tomlin, playing a middle-aged woman going through a mid-life crisis, said, "It was always my goal to be something when I grew up. Now I realize I should have been more specific." The only way we can find a new way up is to be specific and find one way God can use our lives.

A Christian film from New Zealand suggested that we all find a way "To grasp the problems that face our world at the near edge." We can't all do everything. But we can all do one thing. Let's pray God will help us find that one thing, and grasp that problem at the near edge.

Beginning with the Right Question

This brings us to the often perplexing issue of "finding God's will for our lives." There are so many different methodologies Christians use in their attempt to find God's will—from "putting out a fleece" to monitoring circumstances to listening to feelings. I won't discuss the merits of each. Rather, I suggest that as these methodologies are often used, they all suffer from a common flaw. They start with the wrong question.

Let me illustrate. When speaking at a Christian campus, I stated that a popular extracurricular activity of Christian colleges is a little game entitled "Finding the ideal, perfect, private, desirable will of God for my life." This little game begins with the question, "What do I want and what will God let me have?"

Let's say John, a college senior, begins to play. He enters into this negotiation process with God euphemistically called prayer: "Dear God, if you could help me get that high-paying job when I graduate, I would have enough money to get my BMW and the apartment. And, Lord, that woman in my senior class is incredible. If we could work out something there, too. . . ."

After he gets all his ducks in a row, the last question John asks, if at all, is the question of ministry vocation. Picture John out of school and settled in a church. The pastor wonders, "John, now that you're out of school, could you usher for us once in a while?"

"Pastor, no problem. If the slopes aren't good you can count on me. I'll be there."

The point is that you can't get there from here. We can't find God's will for our lives by starting with the self-preoccupied question from the Land of Evermore, "What do I want and what will God let me have?"

The only way to find God's call for our lives is to begin with the kingdom questions, "What does God want? What is God doing in history? How does God want me to be part of what God is doing . . . to make all things new?"

A Prescription for Active Listening

How do we discover how God wants us to be a part of what God is doing in history? I come across so many talented, committed people who have no idea what God is calling them to do. Either God isn't speaking or they aren't listening.

Of course God *is* speaking—inviting and welcoming us to be a part of his loving initiative, the question becomes, How can we become better listeners?

Let me suggest a process of active listening. Even though it has been helpful to some who have tried it, it may not work for everyone. The important thing is that whatever process we follow, we all need to spend more time with Scripture, in prayer, and on active listening to hear from God. And we need to remember that God is sovereign; the working of divine providence is mysterious. We cannot manipulate God's will.

Remember that the moment we became Christians we received our marching orders. We were all called into kingdom service. So the question is not *whether* but *where* God wants us to serve. We also need to remember that God's call is dynamic. As we grow in our gifts and ministry, our sense of vocation will likely change as well.

To set the stage for active listening, I suggest you take a Bible and a journal to a retreat center or someplace you can be alone for a day or more—by yourself or with your spouse. The Catholics have a number of excellent facilities for this purpose that others can use. (Call your local archdiocese for a list.) Begin with your journal open, taking notes as you listen.

1. *Begin with the right question.* Inscribe the right question across the first page of your journal. "Dear God, what are you doing in history? What are your loving purposes, and how do

you want to use my life and gifts to advance your kingdom in the world?" Take ample time to quiet yourself before the Lord so you can be receptive—simply wait.

2. Now, consider: *What is your earliest memory of the call of God in your life?* Journey backward in your story to the time of your earliest Christian experience. Remember those moments when you seemed to sense God calling and challenging your life. Write down in your journal everything you remember of that earliest sense of God's call. Was it a call to work with young people? care for seniors? or minister abroad?

3. *What has God been saying to you through the Bible?* God is constantly nurturing, calling, and chastening us through Scripture. Write in your journal what God has recently been saying to you through the Bible. If you have time, study the kingdom of God in Isaiah and Luke/Acts to get a more compelling sense of God's loving initiative. Or read through chapter three of this book for an overview of God's loving purposes for the world. The more we understand and embrace these purposes as our own, the more effectively they can address our lives.

4. *What has God been saying to you through the needs and suffering of others?* Mother Teresa said it best: "Jesus Christ is thinly disguised in the poor and the suffering of the world." When various human needs—from the plight of children in the *barrios* of Brazil to the trashed lives of teenagers in a suburban strip—grip your heart, that very grip may be God's call on your life, as it was for Elizabeth Fry in chapter four. Write down in your journal all those human conditions, situations, and needs that tug at your life and your heart.

5. *What is God saying to you through your gifts?* You have been gifted for a reason. It isn't simply to increase the profits for IBM or advance the agenda of a professional organization or club. You have been gifted for the kingdom of God. What are your natural gifts in relational, intellectual, mechanical, creative areas? How have you had an opportunity through education and employment to develop those gifts? Write them down in your journal and estimate their stage of development.

Read 1 Corinthians 12. What spiritual gifts has God placed in your life? What opportunities have you had to use these gifts in your church? Write them down.

6. *What is God saying to you through the broken places in your life?* What are some of your areas of weakness and failure? What are problem areas God has been changing? Remarkably, in the economy of God's kingdom God can often do more through our weaknesses than our strengths. Look at Chuck Colson. God has created a marvelous ministry out of Chuck's prison experience. Write down those areas of your life that are the broken places. Ask to be shown how God can transform your weakness into the tools of the kingdom.

7. *What is God saying to you through your imagination?* Invite the Spirit of God to flow through your imagination and help you to discover all kinds of creative ways that everything you have listed thus far can come together. Allow yourself to imagine how that earliest sense of calling and what you hear God saying through Scripture, the needs of others, and your own giftedness and brokenness could converge in whole new possibilities. Use your journal as a dream book. Jot down ideas. Make outlines. Try sketching different clusters of possibilities.

When you are done writing, spend an extended period waiting in silence on the Lord. At the end of your period of silence, jot down any additional impressions God has given you.

You may be surprised what God has to say. God may lead you into more intentional use of your professional training for the kingdom. Or you may feel called into a part-time ministry with internationals in your community. God may challenge you to go overseas on a short-term mission, or to begin a whole new mission in your area. Only God knows what is in store for you.

At this point your initial work is done. You can return home. But your listening isn't over yet. There are more steps to be taken. Over the next few weeks, consider:

8. *What is God saying to you through your active research?* Upon returning from retreat, begin researching the different possibilities you have come up with. If possible, visit those who have already engaged in ministry or vocational activities similar to those you are interested in. If you can't visit, develop a systematic process to write or call such people. Keep a file of all your correspondence. Also write down in your journal what you are learning from your research.

9. *What is God saying to you through community?* Bring everything that you are hearing from God and collecting in research to your small community group. If you haven't found one by this time, try to find two or three mature Christians committed to making a difference in God's kingdom. Share with them the possible new direction you are hearing from God. Ask them for more than a commonsense response; ask them actually to listen with you in prayer for God's confirmation or guidance. Write down what they have to say in your journal, too.

The autonomous individualism that is so much a part of the secular society is also part of our Christian culture—even when it comes to seeking the Lord's guidance. We tend to seek God's will autonomously and privately. Seldom do we listen to God's voice through community. But remember, Paul and Barnabas were called out by community. Once God's vocational call comes into focus in your life and you actually start your partnership in ministry with God, you will still need the community to nurture, support, and encourage you in your new venture.

10. *When is the time to get moving?* Eventually it will be time to take the risk, with the support of those who have been praying with you, to implement your sense of God's call. Begin orchestrating your whole life around your emerging sense of vocation. Reorganize your use of time and resources around your new sense of life purpose. Enjoy the adventure of whole-life stewardship. Now that you have discovered your kingdom vocation "Just do it"!

11. *What is God saying as you continue to listen?* This isn't the conclusion of the listening process; it is only the beginning. You may find it beneficial to go on several retreats to sharpen the listening process. But whatever you do, it is essential that you develop an ongoing active listening process. Even after you find a creative way to express God's vocation through your occupation or your leisure time, you will need to keep listening. I encourage couples and singles to go on prayer retreats at least twice a year to keep their focus sharp.

12. *How should you make decisions in other areas of your life?* As your sense of kingdom vocation comes into focus, it will become your criterion for making decisions in every other area of

life. If God is calling you to be a missionary in Africa, for instance, it makes no sense to marry someone who is firmly committed to staying in the U.S. And if God's call is to work in the inner city, then you probably won't buy a house in the suburbs. All other life decisions need to be made in light of decision #1. Issues such as career, singleness or marriage, and use of time and resources are secondary to the number-one issues—how to link your life to the purposes of God.

Research indicates that those who find the most satisfying way of life have started caring about the needs of others. In fact, it has been found that one of the best therapies for serious depression is reaching out to others. God has built us for caring. The only way we can be fully alive is to devote our lives to the serving purposes of God.

A New Way Up

It's no accident that we've been called on stage during the closing years of the 20th century. We are here for a reason and it's not to get ahead on the job or in the suburbs. Jesus Christ comes challenging us not to make a living but to make a life. Jesus invites us to join with sisters and brothers all over the world in putting God's other serving purposes absolute and first in our lives. That means asking God to transform the direction of our lives from upwardly mobile to outwardly ministerial lives. It means a little word on the job for Jesus won't cut it. It means that every individual and family needs to discover their ministry vocation and take time every week to work with those in need beyond the doors of home and church.

Can you imagine the impact if everyone who claimed to be a follower of Jesus invested one evening a week working with abused kids, young people in drug recovery or neglected seniors? We would begin to see the world turned upside down again by the compassionate power of God unleashed in our lives.

It's showtime. Do you really want to find a more meaningful way of life . . . a way of life that makes a differences . . . a new way up? Then join millions of others who were not content with a business as usual Christianity and put God's purposes first in your life. Discover God's ministry vocation for your life. Free up one evening a week and "just do it."

FOR THOUGHT AND DISCUSSION

1. If you seriously placed God's purposes at the center of your life how would you have to reorder your life?
2. Using the "active listening process," or any other means, try to discern how God wants to use your life in ministry to others.
3. Once you have a clearer sense of your ministry vocation describe how you could reorder your timestyle, your family life or perhaps even your occupation to work intentionally for the purposes of God. When do you plan to start working in your chosen area of research?

LIFE LINKS

life direction	linkages	consequences
Jesus comes inviting us to join him and Christians all over the world in setting aside the self-seeking aspirations of culture in favor of the other service purposes of God. God is, as we have seen, determined to make all things new. And God wants to transform our life direction from upwardly-mobile to outwardly-ministering lives. The Creator God wants to enlist our full participation in all that God is done to bring righteousness, justice, and peace to the earth.	We can either continue to connect our lives to the fraudulent, self-involved aspiration of the culture. Or we can take a risk, with many others, and link our lives to the purposes of God. We can choose to reorder our lives and family around a whole new sense of direction.	If we place God's purposes first in our lives and families . . . if we take time every week to work for God's purposes in our neighborhoods and communities . . . there will be consequences. First our lives will take on new meaning. And as a result of our active ministry, we will see other peoples lives, begin to change as well. We will start to see God's kingdom come and will be done on earth as it is in heaven! We will discover a whole new way to live it up that has more to do with losing than seeking life.

6

Discovering a Life You Can Love

Discovering! With hands outstretched we reach out as infants to discover. And there is no more fundamental discovery than learning how we can be more fully a part of the story of God. I firmly believe the Creator God not only wants us to be a part of making a difference—but wants us to find a way of life *with* a difference.

In the last chapter we talked about the importance of doing, of finding ways actively to advance the purposes of God. In this chapter we want to discuss the importance of being.

The purpose of this chapter is to enable us to find a new way to be in the world . . . a way of life that is a celebrative foretaste of the future of God.

The Struggle to Find a New Way Up

Deep down, I think we all want to find a way to be in the world that is more meaningful and satisfying. But too often we settle for chaotic, disoriented, stressed out lives.

We all have had those terrifying traumatic moments when our entire lives seem to be coming apart at the seams. I remember a traumatic night I spent as a boy of ten at Camp McCoy, near Yosemite. It was the Fourth of July, my first week at camp. We watched fireworks that night until our pupils were dilated large as saucers, then made our way back to the cabin. It was fortunate we all had flashlights. There was no moon, and the combination of dilated pupils and looming blackness would have made the journey impossible without them.

It was an unusually hot night. Like most of the guys in our cabin, I opted to sleep in next to nothing—and on top of my sleeping bag instead of inside.

About two-thirty in the morning, the gallons of soda pop I had consumed in the evening caught up with me. Still in my T-shirt, I stumbled sleepily out of the cabin, but in the darkness I was unable to find the latrine. So I finally did my part to lessen the fire danger for those gigantic sequoias.

Semiconscious and not really able to see anything, I cautiously made my way back to my cabin. I repeatedly ran into trees. Finally, after some twenty minutes, I ran into the cabin.

I felt my way around the perimeter until I violently discovered the stairs with my shins. Not wanting to wake my companions, I kept my screams as muffled as possible. Then, since I couldn't see what I was doing, I crawled into the cabin on my hands and knees and made my way over to my bunk. With tremendous relief, I started to jump back into bed.

Dismay and unbelief! Someone was sleeping in my bunk. As I hung suspended between the bunk and the floor it suddenly dawned on me. I was in the wrong cabin.

This, it occurred to me, could be a very long night. Camp McCoy had almost fifty cabins scattered over three rolling hills.

The rest of the story is almost too painful to relate even at this late date. Through the random encounter method I must have found almost every one of the fifty cabins at least once—plus an interesting assortment of trees, stumps, and ditches. After two hours of this nightmare, I grew seriously frustrated. My skinny body was bruised, skinned, and scraped. And I was getting cold. I felt someone had exiled me on the dark side of the moon without the benefit of clothes, compass, or good sense. And I became almost paralyzed with fear that this aimless wandering would never end.

But my fears as usual were false counselors. Just before dawn I fell over the stairs of a cabin and found the empty bunk I thought I would never see again.

Believe me, I know first hand what it's like to chaotically wander about not knowing which way is up. So I approach empathetically this business of finding a less stressful, more meaningful way of life. Our first task is to try to figure out why our lives are so stressed and meaningless.

Recalling What Brings Us Down

As I mentioned earlier, Louis Harris polls report that 86 percent of Americans report chronic stress. Sixty percent experience chronic stress they do nothing about.

How do we begin to release our stress? Step one is to wake up to the reality that the rat race is a fraud! It's a false way up. It never was the good life. And an entire generation of Christian young, who are programmed to do it all and have it all, are killing themselves in the effort . . . because that dream costs so much more for them, as we have seen, than it did for most of their parents and grandparents.

Part of the blame for the present situation should be placed at the door of the church. Rarely does the church give members any help in getting set free from the stress-race or in redefining the good life. Many churches aren't able to help their members because the churches have so fully embraced modern culture—its values, ambitions, and time-stressed lifestyles are an unquestioned given.

Evangelicals and charismatics talk incessantly of the lordship of Christ over all of life. At the same time, however, these Christians often unquestioningly buy into the individualistic, materialistic, consumer-driven values of the North American culture. They seldom seem to notice the inherent contradiction.

How have we gotten into such a fix? I believe that Christians of all traditions have unwittingly allowed the secular culture to define the aspirations that drive our lives and the values to which we give our lives. In fact, many Christian leaders tend not only to sanction the secular agenda but also to lead the charge toward more upscale, affluent lifestyles.

Rediscovering Whole Discipleship

This spiritualized, culturally captivated Christianity tends to foster a compartmentalized view of discipleship. Compartmentalized discipleship tends to squeeze following Christ into one small spiritual compartment of personal piety and private morality. The other life compartments that have to do with where we work, where we live, how we order our lives, recreate, vacation, shop, and what we value are all largely determined by the secular culture.

The consequences of compartmentalized discipleship are lives virtually indistinguishable from those of our secular neighbors. One reason we are so ineffective in evangelism, I believe, that we are so much like the non-Christians around us; we have little to call them to.

Of course we hang around church buildings a little more than non-Christians. We abstain from a few things. But the fundamental values to which we give our lives just aren't that different. We don't do hedonism as well as those around us but we sure keep trying.

Jesus Christ calls us not to compartmentalized but whole-life discipleship—in which we invite the Creator God to transform every compartment of our lives, not just the spiritual. Looking back to the first century, we see that those first followers weren't involved in compartmentalized discipleship. They weren't doing Roman culture 9:00 to 5:00 with house church on the weekend. They understood, as we don't seem to, that following Jesus Christ is a *whole-life* proposition.

Listen again to the Master calling us away from self-involved lives to follow him with our whole lives.

> Anyone who wishes to be a follower of mine must leave self behind; he must take up his cross, and come with me. Whoever

cares for his own safety is lost; but if a man will let himself be lost for my sake and for the Gospel, that man is safe. What does a man gain by winning the whole world at the cost of his true self? (Mark 8:34-36, NEB)

Christ's call to discipleship is clear. Either we follow him with our entire lives or we risk missing life. Author John Alexander explains why so many of us, including church leaders, tend to draw back.

Christians spend a lot of time and energy explaining why Jesus couldn't possibly have meant what he said. This is understandable; Jesus was an extremist and we are all moderates. What's worse he was an extremist in his whole life—not just in the narrowly spiritual areas—but in everything, so we have to find ways to dilute his teachings.[1]

Once we understand that following Jesus is a whole-life proposition, we can never go back to a more moderate, disengaged, compartmentalized discipleship. If we are to find the more meaningful way of life for which God created us, then we must go forward into the adventure of whole-life discipleship.

Whole-Life Discipleship: Fleshing Out the Future of God

In the last chapter we discussed the importance of inviting God to transform our life direction so we can be much more actively involved in working for God's purposes in the world. However, I don't believe the first call of the gospel is to proclamation—and I believe very strongly in the importance of evangelism. Nor do I believe the first call of the gospel is to social action—yet we certainly need more ministry with the poor and forgotten.

I believe the first call of the gospel is to incarnation. Only as we flesh out, in community, something of God's new order will we have any authentic basis from which to proclaim or demonstrate the gospel of Jesus Christ.

In other words, whole-life discipleship begins with being, not doing. Catholics remind us that we are called to sacramentally be the presence of Christ in the world . . . grounded in the life of prayer. They are right. Charismatics and Pentecostals are also right when they insist we must be filled with the Spirit of the living God. There is no way, of course, we can as whole-life disciples manifest the fruits of the Spirit unless the Spirit of Christ dwells in us.

But whole-life disciples must not only be filled by the Spirit of God. We must also be filled with God's loving vision for a future made new. A few Mennonite authors have been writing about whole-life discipleship for a number of years. While much evangelical literature on discipleship draws heavily on the Pauline epistles, Mennonite authors emphasize the gospels—the life and teachings of Jesus Christ.

For example, Donald Kraybill in his important book, *The Upside-Down Kingdom,* calls us to a much more radical brand of Christian discipleship. He calls us to a gospel in which losers are winners, the last are first, and dying is living. Kraybill correctly insists that gospel discipleship requires that God not only change our hearts but transform our values so we live out the right-side-up values of God's kingdom in an upside-down world. Kraybill asks what our lifestyles would look like if we struggled to flesh out the beatitudes of Jesus in our daily lives as those first disciples did.[2] (However, I am disappointed at how many Mennonites seem unable to discern the difference between the radical biblical discipleship of their own literature and the more trivialized spiritualized, compartmentalized, superficial discipleship promoted through popular Christian literature and media.)

Whole-life Discipleship: A New Community of Life

What does whole-life discipleship look like? How is it different from simply doing the American dream with a little Jesus overlay? If we as whole-life disciples are to flesh out something that looks more like the kingdom than the culture, where do we begin?

Jesus Christ came proclaiming a single message—"good

new, good news that the future of God has broken into our midst!" Christ came not only proclaiming the inbreaking of the future of God, he also demonstrated it.

Jesus Christ was not only the full disclosure of Creator God, he and that first community were a foretaste of the coming kingdom of God. They expressed a way of being in the world that had more of the aroma of the kingdom than the culture.

Instead of giving ourselves unquestioningly to the values and aspirations of the secular culture, Jesus calls us as whole disciples to flesh out his good news. But we can only do that in community. Listen to Michael Green's description of the earliest community and the way they fleshed out the values of God's kingdom that were clearly counter to the values of the dominant culture at that time.

> They made the grace of God credible by a society of love and mutual care which astonished pagans and was recognized as something entirely new. It lent persuasiveness to their claim that the new age had dawned in Christ. The Word was not only announced but seen in the community of those who were giving it flesh.
>
> The message of the kingdom became more than an idea. A new human community had sprung up and looked very much like new order to which the evangelist had pointed. Here love was given daily expression; reconciliation was actually occurring; people were no longer divided into Jew and Gentiles, slave and free, male and female. In this community the weak were protected, the stranger welcomed. People were healed, the poor and dispossessed were cared for and found justice. Everything was shared. Joy abounded and ordinary lives were filled with praise.[3]

Over the past two millennium, millions of other Christians have discovered the joy of fleshing out in community something that looks more like God's new order. From Celtic and Franciscan monasteries to Moravian communities and Wesleyan holy clubs, many of those who have gone before us have found a new way of being in the world that has always challenged the validity of the dominant culture.

Whole-life Discipleship:
Creating Communities of the Kingdom

Today there are still thousands of Christians living in Catholic and Protestant orders seeking to flesh out something of the presence of God's new future. And thousands of others have created broad spectrum of other forms of Christian community.

A New Way Up with the Bruderhof

I want to introduce you to 290 people living in a residential community in Woodcrest, New York, called the Bruderhof (a community of Hutterites which immigrated to the U.S. from Germany almost 100 years ago). They work conscientiously at living out the right-side-up values of God's kingdom in an upside-down world.

Seldom have I seen Christians anywhere do a better job of raising children than those at the Bruderhof. Their children are raised in a community in which there is no fragmentation, addiction, or abuse. And while each family has a private household in Bruderhof apartments, the entire community operates like one large extended family. Everyone is involved in helping raise the children, including seniors and even older children.

The entire community reads Scripture, sings, and prays together every night as one common evening meal is shared in the dining room. Family life isn't bonded through consumerism but through service. The children are not surrounded by their own private stereos, TVs, VCRs, and phones. At Christmas each child receives only one small present instead of being inundated with things.

The most important thing Bruderhof families do together is not to hang out at the malls or go on expensive outings. The major bonding in family life comes from parents and kids working with offenders in a prison near their community and going into New York City on a regular basis to work with the poor and the homeless. These good people have created a new way of being in the world that is not only simpler and less stressed but more satisfying. Such living clearly reflects something of the compassion of God's kingdom.

The Bruderhof is a common purse community, which means incomes are pooled and a communal way of life similar to that of the first Christians is created. As a consequence this type of Christian community is not within reach for many Christians.

But for those of us determined to be whole-life disciples, community really isn't optional. It is essential. And spilling coffee on one another Sunday morning isn't community. So for those who aren't ready for a communal option, what are the alternatives? What are options beyond the community we experience in our nuclear families?

First, in view of all the discussion of "family values," some clarifications are in order. The nuclear family didn't come with the ark of covenant. When the Bible discusses the family, it isn't talking about the modern nuclear family, which has been around less than 100 years. It is talking about a more traditional extended family, which includes a broad spectrum of grandparents, aunts, uncles, and more.

The teaching on the family we don't hear over Christian radio or in popular Christian media is that the church is called to be God's new family. Remember when someone came up to Jesus and said, "Hey, your mother and brother are over here," Jesus responded, "Who is my mother or brother but he who does the will of God?" Jesus wasn't minimizing the importance of biological relationships but he *was* drawing a new, larger, inclusive circle. Those of us who are sisters and brothers in Christ are called to be part of a new family.

A New Way Up at West Hills Covenant

What that means at a local level is that we really need to find ways to be God's family together. At West Hills Covenant Church in Portland, Oregon, for example, the entire congregation has been divided into face-to-face groups. These small groups, which meet weekly, include nuclear families as well as single parents and those widowed or divorced. In addition to studying Scripture and praying together, they really operate like extended families. They visit one another in the hospital, they share meals together, they share vehicles, and they are there for one another in times of crisis.

The leaders of these small groups meet with pastoral leadership on a regular basis in what they call the "servant's staff." In these meetings they share about those who are in trouble and those who are moving ahead in their Christian life. They draw on the resources of the whole body to care for members who are in need. These small groups equip members to reach beyond the congregation family to those in need in the community. In the way they care for one another and those in their community, these Christians have found a new way to be in the world that is genuinely a foretaste of the new family of God.

Creating Your Own Way Up

For most of us probably the easiest way to become a part of God's new community is in a small group that meets once a week. However, the extent to which we can express something of God's kingdom values is limited by the amount of time we spend together and our geographical proximity.

Creating a New Way Up Through Co-op Communities

Those of us serious about whole-life discipleship have the opportunity to create a whole new spectrum of other modes of Christian community. My wife and I purchased a triplex in Seattle with the intention of creating a cooperative residential Christian community in which each family has a separate household. Because of our proximity to the other two families, we hope to have more time to create one small alternative to the North American stress-race.

A group of Seattle Mennonites are also seriously exploring selling their single family detached homes in the suburbs and using the equity to jointly purchase an urban apartment house. Goals include reducing the amount of money spent on shelter as well as creating a new cooperative community that reflects something of the values of God's new order.

We in the church have embraced single family detached living as an unquestioned given . . . failing to recognize the inherent autonomy and alienation of this model. And increasing the Christian young can no longer afford it. We need some whole new housing and community options for the next generation.

Huge mortgage payments are a major life stress for many couples. I run into many young couples who are working not only two full-time jobs but increasingly three full-time jobs to buy the single family detached and everything that goes with it. Not surprisingly, these folks are lucky to make it to church. They are running so fast they don't have time left for service, prayer, or community.

We are called by Scripture and may be forced by the economy to find new ways to cooperate together. I think we will, if belatedly, discover that the do your own thing lifestyle is highly overrated. I believe cooperatives are the wave of the future.

For example, a group of Mennonites in Langley, B.C., developed a mortgage cooperative called the lamp program. They paid an amount beyond their regular mortgages to a cooperative mortgage fund. Then they paid off member's mortgages based on their need. Those people then continued to pay into the common fund. To everyone's surprise, mortgages of all members were paid off in only seven years through this creative, cooperative model. They found a new way up.

As we enter a new century, we will need to create a broad spectrum of new housing cooperatives and communities. Thousands of people in Denmark opted out of single family lifestyles years ago. They weren't religiously motivated. They were simply convinced that cooperative living was superior.

For example, one cooperative in Denmark, built like a condo, houses seventy-five people. There are one-bedroom to four-bedroom units. They are built modestly. Instead of everyone having a recreation room, there is one large recreation area for the entire complex. For those who want them, meals are available in the rec center in the evenings for $1.00 per person. And every couple cooks once every two months.

Instead of private back and front yards, the co-op has one cooperative area for the kids to play and one cooperative area for residents to garden. Danes living in this community report preferring this cooperative way of life—in which they share childcare, gardening, and even family celebrations with their neighbors—over the alienation of being on their own.

With LeRoy Troyer's help I have created, on paper, one modest variation on this cooperative theme that could provide an opportunity for Christians to flesh out something of God's kingdom in a creative new model. I propose we help Christians, particularly the Christian young, to build cooperative sixplexes.

I suggest we enable, for example, six young couples to build six three bedroom, one-bath homes clustered on a third of an acre lot. As in the Danish co-ops, units would share common recreation, laundry, and storage rooms. The six units would be clustered around a central courtyard where kids could play. And the land surrounding the housing cluster could be used for a cooperative garden, complete with edible vegetation.

These units could be built in many parts of the country for about $60,000 a unit, including the land and the shared areas. I propose that those in the church who are older and more affluent provide no-interest loans for those buying into this sixplex. (They would get their principal back in five years, having lost only the interest.)

So instead of spending a half-million dollars over thirty years for a $150,000 house, these couples would spend $60,000 over five years for a $60,000 house. The six couples could pay two additional years beyond payout to advance God's kingdom. That would free up $144,000, which could be used to build 100 homes for the poor overseas or five to six Habitat for Humanity houses in the U.S.

At the end of the seventh year, the six couples would have no mortgage payments. Therefore they would no longer have to work at two full-time jobs. Each couple could chose to work at two half-time jobs or could rotate full time work. Then they would not only have more time for their children but time to work for the purposes of God. "Sight for the blind, release to the captives, and good news for the poor!"

Apart from the obvious economic benefits of such cooperative living, there is the opportunity to create an imaginative new kind of Christian community. A new way to be in the world.

The six couples could have the advantage of proximity without communalism. Each family would have its own home while sharing a few common areas and the opportunity for a more co-operative way of life.

The six couples could gather once a week, not just to study and pray, but to create a common life together that looked more like the kingdom than the suburban rat race. They could create a festive new model of life together that would give us all a glimpse of what the future of God will look like.

I encourage all those serious about whole-life discipleship to find others with whom to create a small covenant group where they can express a new way of being in the world. We all need to be a part of communities where we are truly known, loved, and held accountable. Only in community can we become whole-life disciples and begin to discover, with others, a more meaningful way of life. I encourage those up to the challenge to consider creating a more intentional cooperative community, regardless of whether it looks like sixplex, a rural prayer retreat center, or cooperative apartment house community.

Whether we are a part of a small group or a cooperative community, all our communities will benefit from direct con-nection to a traditional church, which can provide accountabili-ty and support. And as we begin this journey into community, I encourage us all to visit Christian communities in our areas to see the broad range of what God is already creating.

Whole-Life Discipleship: Biblically Discovering a New Way Up

Once we find a group of Christians with whom we can be in community, then we can begin the adventure of applying Scrip-ture to all of life—particularly the neglected part, our values and aspirations. How do we do this? Let me suggest one way.

I propose that you and your small group do Bible study through the Gospel of Luke. The purpose of this study is to de-termine how the aspirations and values of Christ and his king-dom differ from the aspirations and values of the secular cul-ture in which we have been raised. Then as whole-life disciples we can invite the Spirit of God not only to change our hearts and heal our psychological hangups, but also to transform our life directions and values.

Make four lists—two lists before you begin the study; one while you study the Gospel; and one after the study is over.

1. First have everyone in your group list aspirations and values of the dominant culture as you experience them. Particularly try to identify the notion of the better future implicit in those values. This list will probably contain aspirations like *moving on up, getting a piece of the rock, lifestyles of the rich and famous.* Note that North American culture tends to define the better future in largely economic and materialistic terms. Additional values listed may include *doing our own thing, individual freedom, privacy, consumerism, affluence, status, power, achievement, self-interest, hedonism, etc.*

2. Second, have persons in your group privately and *honestly* list which aspirations and values from the list on the dominant culture are also their own. Specifically ask people to discern, based on how they use their own time and money, what's important to them. Their list may include getting ahead in their careers, getting ahead in the suburbs, privacy, security, personal freedom, or having an occasional shopping binge.

3. Third, as you and your group study Luke, keep a cooperative list of the aspirations and values that appear to be a part of the life and teachings of Christ and of the first Christians. I suspect your group will discover that the aspirations of Jesus Christ and the first community are directly connected to the story of God and God's vision for a world made new that we experienced together in chapter 3. And your group will also likely discover that the aspirations and values Jesus Christ calls us to are paradoxical, radical, and clearly counterpoint to many of the values of the dominant culture.

Christ calls us not to seek life but to lose life. Instead of seeking to be served, we are called to serve. I suspect we will discover that Christ's definition of the good life has more to do with the celebration of relationships, time spent with the Creator God, and the joy of giving life away.

Pay attention during the study to the values expressed in the way Jesus prioritized his life. We usually find Jesus in one of two places—either with God or with people, healing, loving, teaching, celebrating.

Your list of values discovered in the life and teachings of Christ might include going the second mile, loving enemies, forgiving friends, hanging out with the outcasts, hugging kids, giving away power, washing feet, challenging the established order, restoring lives, and celebrating at weddings. The gospel calls us away from our rampant individualisms into the kind of community we witness Jesus sharing with the twelve. The gospel is also revealed through the intentionally simple way of life Jesus and the first community modeled so they could be present with the poor and unencumbered by economic demands.

4. As the study of Luke concludes, ask each person again to make a private list. This time ask participants *honestly* to list what values of Christ are genuinely part of our lives.

We will all wind up on two lists. Then we can invite the Spirit of God not only to change our hearts and help us with our hang-ups and relationships but also to begin transforming the aspirations that direct our lives and the fundamental values that order our lives. Only as we begin, in community, to invite God to change all compartments of our lives do we have any possibility of becoming whole life disciples.

And this study will also enable us to begin biblically redefining what the good life really is. The good life of God has more to do with the celebration of relationships than the acquisition of things. It has more to do with losing than with seeking life. God has a new way of life for us that is more festive and celebrative than anything the rat race can offer.

Whole-Life Discipleship: Beginning the Adventure in a Life of Prayer

Once we clarify the new way of life Scripture calls us to, the journey toward whole-life discipleship can begin earnestly—in prayer. The only way we can flesh out something of God's new future is through God's Spirit dwelling in us. And the way we meet the Spirit is through the life of prayer.

This adventure begins as we encounter the living God in the mystery of the bread and wine, in the quiet places of listening, and through meditating and praying in prayer retreats. If Christ needed to go on prayer retreats, we certainly need to. As whole-life disciples we need to transform our timestyles so we have significant time for prayer and meditating on the Word of God.

Meditating on Scripture will remind us that the Creator loves us dearly and through the grace of Christ has redeemed us. Key to the life of prayer is the recognition that our God delights in us and wants to share greater intimacy with each of God's children. Therefore, at the very center of creating a life we can love is taking significant time to draw close to our God so the Holy Spirit will transform us into the likeness of Jesus.

For many families, the major time of praying together comes at bedtime, when children say their prayers and parents listen. Children's bedtime prayers can be valuable as the beginning of a lifetime prayer habit. And they can remind us that we are encouraged to come to God about every need in our lives as well as with the needs of others. You might enjoy this little humorous piece written by my sister-in-law, Karen Sine, about children's night prayers, in a Catholic family:

Children pray, "Matthew, Mark, Luke, and John, bless this bed that I lie on," and the evangelists, abruptly summoned from rapture, dash wildly to earth for bed blessing. On the way they dodge flights of angels and assorted saints. Between the hours of eight and nine at night, when children say their prayers, Christianity is an extremely hectic religion.

The Medieval philosophers have suffered considerable snide criticism for wasting their time estimating how many angels could dance on the head of a pin. The climate of modern thought does not support the spectacle of any angels whatever, let alone merry ones dancing. Yet there they are on a hot night, roosting on bedposts in a cluttered room with a gang of saints, taking notes:

"Please find my walrus, Boomer. I can't go to sleep without him." That's an easy one. Get St. Anthony for the walrus. "Bless the whales." Whales? Who's got whales? Oh, good ole Jonah, he hates whales. Give the whales to Jonah.

". . . all the ships at sea and the planes in the air." Elmo, Christopher, Raphael. That should do it.

"And bless our country." Where are we? Oh, anybody here got the United States? Yes, all of it. (Powers, thrones, dominions take the U.S.) Good luck.

"Bless the bad people and get their heads chopped off." Hmm. Sounds like Simon Peter. He likes whacking people.

"Bless our house." Cuthman? No you have churches. Joseph, you take the house like a good fellow, and do something about that porch. Somebody is going to get killed.

"And bless Mommy and Daddy." Silence. The archangels shrink from parenthood. They stare appraisingly at the saints who shuffle, sneeze, cough, rattle, blush, shrug, and check one another for lint. Hilary? Charles? Cosmas or Damien?

Pass

How about you, Francis? You always like martyrdom. I've got sharks this week. You take them. But it's only two people this time, a man and a woman. Happily married, too. Fear not.

Ha. That's what they all say.

Now, who had Mommy and Daddy last time? Nobody since Christopher, and he's been defrocked; lost his feast day over it. I'm not going to take them. Something always happens. Every night the same old thing. How about God the Father? (Wild applause). Well done, Aquinas! That settles it. Mothers and fathers to God Almighty. Lights flick out. A child sighs to sleep, clutching a wet walrus St. Anthony found in the vaporizer.

However one feels about saints, angels, or parenthood, children's bedtime prayers can be valuable as the beginning of a lifetime prayer habit. And they can remind us that we are encouraged to come to God about every need in our lives, as well as the needs of others.

But of course there is more to prayer than petitioning—asking God for ourselves or someone else. Prayer also involves contemplation, meditation, and solitude. We have much to learn in this regard from our Catholic friends, who have a long history of emphasizing a life of prayer. But Protestants too are experiencing a growing hunger for a deeper spirituality. Books by Henri Nouwen, Thomas Merton, and Richard Foster—all advocates of a life of prayer and spiritual discipline—are becoming increasingly common on Protestant bookshelves. This reflects a growing longing by both Protestants and Catholics to be more profoundly linked to God and God's story for their lives.

Thomas Merton writes, "The union of the Christian with Christ is a mystical union in which Christ himself becomes the source and principle of life in me. Christ Himself . . . 'breathes' in me divinely in giving me his Spirit."[4]

And Henri Nouwen explains,

> There is probably no image that expresses so well the intimacy with God in prayer as the image of God's breath. . . . We receive a new breath of freedom, a new life. This new life is the divine life of God himself. Prayer, therefore, is God breathing in us, by which we become part of the intimacy of God's inner life and by which we are born anew.
>
> So the paradox of prayer is that for serious effort while it can only be received as a gift. We cannot plan, organize or manipulate God, but without a careful discipline we cannot receive him either.[5]

A growing number of Christians realize that to genuinely became a part of God's story they must first become a part of God's life. And they see that to receive something of the gift of God's life requires more discipline than most of us know anything about. It means more than quickly praying, "God bless Mom and Dad" and off to bed or work. We must develop a life of prayer centered in God.

A Modest Proposal for a New Way Up Through Prayer

To become whole-life disciples we must take significant time for prayer. Here are suggestions for a discipline of prayer that come out of my own journey.

1. Find a regular time and place for your spiritual disciplines and protect it. Aim to spend at least thirty minutes a day in prayer and study, then try to work toward an hour a day.
2. Learn to center your attention on God—not on your problems. Quiet your spirit before God. Release to the Creator God all the things that fill your mind. I am having to learn to do this. My prayer life used to be totally wrapped up in my problems, and I was getting nowhere. But now I am learning to focus on God, and it is changing my prayer life.
3. Use the format of the Lord's Prayer for your own praying. Begin by praising God, then pray for the accomplishment of God's kingdom purposes. Pray in response to the needs of others before you pray for your own needs. Pray that God will bind the power of darkness and release God's renewing Spirit in the world. Remember we must learn to forgive any toward whom we feel resentment.
4. Use Richard Foster's book, *The Celebration of Discipline,* as an aid in learning how to meditate, contemplate, and focus on God in your prayer life. Learn to use your imagination in study, meditation, and prayer. Picture yourself present during events in Scripture and invite God to minister to you.
5. Find someone whose life is given to prayer to teach you more about the spiritual disciplines—to be a "soul friend." Spend time with that person at least twice a month, learning about spirituality and a life of prayer.
6. Develop a systematic program of reading through the Bible. Also study your way more carefully through a single book. For example, try going through the book of Isaiah, underlining every portion that refers to the loving purposes of God for the human future and meditating on the imagery. Memorize Scripture passages important to your life.
7. Go on retreats at least twice a year, taking nothing but a Bible

and a journal. This is a practice I find helpful. As I read the Word and wait in silence before the Lord, I always gain new direction for my life. I also find it helpful to spend time every Sunday journaling and evaluating how consistently I live out God's call on my life. This process might also help you focus your life and later your values and priorities to bring them in line with the kingdom. My wife and I find this as also a good time to check in and pray together.

Whole-Life Discipleship:
Creating a Timestyle and a Lifestyle You Can Love

The Kingdom of God Is a Party shouts from the cover of one of Tony Campolo's books. Tony is right. If we redefine our notion of the good life so it looks more like the celebrative future of God instead of the stress-race, we can begin life over again.

In the 1970s there was much literature on Christian lifestyle change which called for a spiraling downward economic mobility that seemed destined to end in abject poverty. (At least that was the way it came across to many.) As a consequence such literature wasn't easy to market and had little staying power.

In this book we are emphasizing lifestyle change as primarily cultural not economic. This means we have the opportunity to simplify lives but also to create a range of imaginative new options. I encourage people to begin changing their lifestyles not by giving up anything but rather by adding celebration to their lives.

Whole-Life Stewardship:
Living It Up with Renewed Celebration

We can do better than Trivial Pursuit, Nintendo, and Madonna. We can take charge of every part of our lives, call our own *tunes*, create our own party times.

Our Jewish friends have the right idea. They don't relate to their faith solely through didactic teaching situations. They vitally engage their faith through celebrations of remembrance. A small child's question annually begins the celebration of Passover. Friends and I have enriched our lives and faith over the years celebrating Jewish celebrations of Passover, the feast of Booths, and Pentecost. If you haven't tried these celebrations, wait no longer. They are part of your heritage too. And messianic Jews in your community would, I am sure, be glad to help start celebrating the acts of God in our past.

But we aren't limited to celebrations of remembrance. As Christians we can create whole new celebrations of anticipation. Plan a party with a difference. Organize it around a biblical theme that resonates with joy, that anticipates the new future of God.

Consider creating a party around the kingdom of God as a wedding feast, Jubilee, or around the Great Homecoming Banquet of God. If you were going to create a celebration of the wedding feast of God's kingdom, what activity, music, and Scripture would you incorporate in the celebration? How would you help your friends get a taste of what you are looking forward to?

Recently a small group of us in Seattle created a party around the theme, "Advent II: Homecoming." Advent I was when Christ came to us in Bethlehem. Advent II is when we will all come home to the future of God—a world made new. At the second advent of Jesus Christ, people from every tongue and tribe and nation will come home to the mountain of God, celebrating a world restored.

We invited about forty people, most of whom didn't know each other, to this celebration. The first thing we asked people to do was share their most poignant memories of homecoming. One man shared what it was like to come back alive from Vietnam when most of his buddies did not. A young woman shared the joy of coming home to the welcome in her mother's eyes.

We read the passage from Isaiah about the children of Israel coming home from their captivity in Babylon to their beloved city of David. Next we sang Jewish choruses as if we were the ones actually on the way home to Jerusalem, experiencing all the joy and anticipation those Jewish refugees must have felt. And it began to become more up-tempo.

Then I announced, "Now we are going to dance into the

streets of Jerusalem!" Terror in the eyes of these Presbyterians, people who had never moved their bodies in their entire lives. They started edging toward the door, but the door was locked and bolted. We had invited a Jewish folk dance instructor. Now we turned on the Jewish folk dance music. For the first fifteen minutes it was painful to watch those rigid bodies. But soon every one loosened up. We began dancing like we were coming home to Jerusalem to a future made new . . . to a celebration of restoration, justice, and peace.

Then we shared a festive buffet with dishes from Africa, Asia and Latin America—because the homecoming of God is going to be a wonderful cross-cultural banquet. We ate until we were stuffed. Finally, we ended our evening as we will begin our homecoming, with the bread and wine of the Eucharist.

Some people are creating new family rituals and rites of passage. One group came up with the idea of a seven-day celebration of creation. Students at Goshen had a manna party. To get in you had to bring whatever represented life-sustaining manna to you. Another group celebrated All Saint's Day with a costume party honoring those who have gone before us. Still others simply celebrated people they cared about with no good reason at all.

You see, even when it comes to celebration we can do better than passively allowing the secular culture to entertain us. We can actively create our own good times and even teach our young how to really party hearty!

Whole-Life Stewardship: Creating a Timestyle You Can Love

The most chronic problem I run into in the church today is people who are out of control in their timestyles. For some of us our busyness is fed by the need to perform and achieve. We live for the strokes we receive from our activity-addicted lives. For some our drivenness is messianic.

A pastor once told me, "Tom, this business of dying for the kingdom has been done once already. It doesn't have to be done again." Many in Christian service have substituted activity for being. We have mistakenly assumed that God's kingdom won't come unless we kill ourselves with frenetic activity. But a lot of us are too busy simply because we have never paused long enough to reflect on what's important, on how we should be in the world.

In every age and time God wants to set the captives free from whatever makes us captive—including busyness-consumed lives. God wants to help us all find a new way of being, a timestyle with an easier rhythm and a clearer sense of what's important.

For those truly addicted to achievement, and strokes for frenetic activity, the way back probably has to begin with serious counseling. In one of my creativity workshops, some young people actually came up with an imaginative proposal for a Twelve-step program for time-addicted Christians. I know a lot of people who could benefit from such a program.

I used to be a type "A" person myself. I met myself coming and going; I was booked every night of the week. Then during a trip to Haiti, Haitian friends took us to visit with a different family in the village each evening. We would tell stories, sing, and eat. I couldn't remember when I last had simply taken time to be with people in the states.

I came back from Haiti and freed up one evening a week, then two. Now I have six nights a week free. My Haitian friends helped me discover a new rhythm, a better way of life, and the joy of taking time to be present to those I care about. I have no desire to go back to the fast track. I've found a new way up.

Would you like to be free from the fast track? The answer isn't a time management course. The change begins as we just discussed—by biblically redefining what constitutes the good life. Then we need to reorder our timestyles to reflect our new sense of purpose and our reordered values, our new biblical definition of the good life.

I suggest we begin this journey toward reordered timestyles by clearing the decks. Try to cancel every time commitment you can reasonably let go of, even if only it means freeing up one evening a week. Then resist the temptation to fill the open time with anything. Simply savor your free time and use it to celebrate life and those you care about.

After you have freed up as much time as you can, retreat. Take a weekend and retreat with your spouse or by yourself to seek God's help to reorder your life. My wife and I do this four times a year. Ponder these questions:

1. How much time should we set aside for daily prayer, contemplation and Bible study?
2. How much time should we provide each week to be a part of a small group and genuinely share community not only with family but those God calls us to be together with?
3. How much time should we invest in ministry to others? How much time should we take every week to work for God's purposes in the world?
4. How much time do we want to share with our family and friends in the celebration and worship of our loving God? Time in creative new celebrations of God's kingdom?

I realize there are those in nursing homes and others raising small children who don't have as many timestyle options. But most of us with a little effort and imagination can create timestyles both less pressured and more celebrative. With others, we can find a new way to be in the world that makes a difference. Most of us can create a timestyle we really love.

Whole-Life Stewardship: Creating a Lifestyle You Can Love

One dramatic way we can free up time is to reduce lifestyle costs. For example, if we can reduce the amount we spend on housing, then we won't have to spend so much time working and we will be able to spend that time on things that matter. Earlier we mentioned cooperative living. Here is another option.

John and Pam did the hard biblical work of redefining what the good life was for their family. This led them to ask how much floor space they really needed with two little boys. Unlike many older Christian couples who opted for huge houses and matching mortgages, John and Pam decided they would themselves build a more modest two-bedroom split-level home—and do it without a mortgage.

Four years ago they completed construction. They are now enjoying their new beautiful home in Redmond, Washington. It has a living room, dining room, kitchen, small den, sun porch, and upstairs two bedrooms and a bath. Their home has the most attractive cabinetry I have seen. Total cost for the materials to construct their own home? $25,000.

What's the difference between $25,000 front end cash and a half-million dollars over thirty years for a $150,000 house? A whole lot of two people's lives! Through this brand of whole-life stewardship, John and Pam found a new way up. As a result of building their own home, Pam was able to quit her job. Now she has more time to spend with her boys and also more time to become involved in the ministries of the local Mennonite church. And John can take off work periodically to do short-term video work overseas for World Concern. Through whole-life stewardship . . . this family found a new way up.

Not everyone can build their own home, of course. But we can all find imaginative ways to create lifestyles that are both more festive and less consumptive. We can all cut down on un-necessary expenditures, get out of debt, and pay off credit cards to save on high interest rates. We all need to ask, "How much is enough?" How much do we really need to spend on housing, transportation, food, wardrobe, recreation, dining out, and va-cations, while in other parts of the world Christians can't keep their kids fed? There is something desperately wrong in the body of Christ when some of us live palatially and others don't live at all.

One couple found a creative way to cut back on vacation costs. They arranged a two-week house swap with friends in an-other state. They had a great vacation for a modest cost.

A group of five Christian couples who used to go out to eat together once a month found a creative alternative. Now they take turns having festive international meals in one another's homes once a month. They have fun decorating their house around a national theme, cooking a complete dinner from their chosen country, and sharing some information about that coun-try and God's work there. After each monthly celebration they take the $200 they would have spent eating out and invest it in a mission project in their chosen country.

Still others have cut back on giving expensive gifts and have chosen to make gifts or to give time, such as to a fishing trip with a child. My wife has knit me a beautiful sweater which I cherish much more than anything that comes from a store.

Some argue that if they reduce expenditures on expensive cars, second homes, or wardrobes, it will have no impact on anyone else. That isn't true. If we free up $20,000 or $20 and invest the money in a mission project or on economic improvement among the poor, it will have a decisive impact on the lives of those in need. The missing stewardship teaching in the church is that we live in an interdependent, interconnected world. If we use more than a fair share of God's resources, someone in this world is going to go without. It is still true that we need to "learn to live simply that others might simply live."

As we enter a new century, it will be essential for all of us to adopt much more cooperative lifestyles, not only because of the mandate of Scripture but also because of the changing economic realities in our world. We will need to create food co-ops, housing co-ops, and ways to cooperatively care for one another —particularly the children, the seniors, and the marginalized in our midst.

Those of us who embark on the adventure of creating more festive, less demanding lifestyles need to be reminded we can't do it alone. We need the support and accountability of community. For example, Assembly Mennonite in Elkhart, Indiana, has broken the entire congregation into small, face-to-face groups. Like other covenant groups, they study Scripture together and pray for one another. Like extended families, they also care for one another, share resources, and seek to reflect in their life together something of the values of God's new order.

Twice a year each small group comes together to help each member prayerfully reflect on timestyle and lifestyle priorities. During these special meetings, all members of each small group open their time schedules and budgets to everyone in their small group. In this way they seek God's stewardship and discernment through those with whom they are in community.

This model reminds me of the accountability that apparently

was part of that earliest Christian community. And this kind of accountability is essential if we are to be whole life disciples and stewards in *a world that relentlessly seeks to seduce us to give ourselves to frenetic schedules and mindless consumerism.*

Whole-Life Stewardship:
A Look Backward and a Look Forward

In this chapter we have argued that the first call of the gospel is not to doing but to being. We are invited to discover a new way to be in the world that looks more like the celebrative future of God than the North American stress-race. This new way of being requires that we jettison our culturally captivated compartmentalized discipleship in favor of a whole-life discipleship that includes redefining the good life. The only way we can be whole-life disciples is in community with other sisters and brothers . . . really participating in extended families, where we are known and loved and held accountable. This new incarnational way of being in the world is deeply rooted in the life of prayer and filled with the presence of God's Spirit.

You are invited to join sisters and brothers all over the world in discovering a new way of being . . . together creating a life you can truly love.

FOR THOUGHT AND DISCUSSION

In preparation for discovering vocational direction in the next chapter, let's review the following questions:

1. What Christians and groups do you know who really reflect the unique festive presence of God's new future in our world today?
2. How do you want God to change your values into kingdom values? What specific values do you want to change first?
3. What specific ways are you considering moving more seriously into whole-life discipleship, a life of prayer, and a life joined with others to reflect the joyful presence of God? Write down ideas for adding more celebration to your life, intensity to your prayers, intentionality to your community.

Compartmentalized Discipleship	Whole-Life Discipleship
In the conventional view, Christian discipleship is compartmentalized. God comes in and transforms our hearts and sometimes even heals our psychological hang-ups. But our life direction and values remain untouched. What was our life direction before we became Christians? Upward mobility. What was our life direction after we became Christians? Upward mobility. The only difference is that now we have God to help us. What were our life values before we became Christians? Materialism, individualism, and looking out for #1. After conversion? The same. Since the core of our lives is devoted to the culture around us, the things of faith tend to be shoved into little compartments at the periphery of our lives. This view trivializes what it means to be followers of Jesus in our world.	Those first Christians weren't doing Roman culture nine to five with a house church on weekends! They understood that it is impossible to accept Jesus into our hearts without accepting his mission purposes into our lives. Jesus Christ doesn't come just to change hearts and heal psychological hang-ups. He also wants to transform our life direction from upward mobility to outward mobility and outward ministry. Jesus wants to change our values from those of culture to those of the kingdom of God. When the core of our life is transformed by the power of God, everything begins to change—the way we house ourselves, the way we celebrate—everything! We orchestrate our whole lives around the kingdom purposes of God. This is whole-life discipleship, which takes seriously Jesus' call to follow him and really make him Lord of all life.

7

Sharing Life Beyond the Doors of Home and Church

S haring! As children, we show we are growing up when we begin to be able to look beyond ourselves and share with others. As members of families, we learn to share life with those we love. And as we are grafted into the family of God, we learn to share ourselves and our resources beyond anything we believed possible. We even learn to share in response to urgent needs of people beyond our families and churches—as an extension of God's love in our world.

The purpose of this chapter is to enable local congregations to become more active and creative in sharing God's love beyond the doors of home and church.

Of course we know we are supposed to share ourselves with friends and family. But listen to Jesus' challenge to us to move toward caring for everyone—even our enemies.

If you love those who love you, what credit is that to you? Even "sinners" love those who love them. And if you do good to those who are good to you, what credit is that to you? Even "sinners" do that. And if you lend to those from whom you expect repayment, what credit is that to you? Even "sinners" lend to "sinners," expecting to be repaid in full. But love your enemies, do good to them, and lend to them without expecting to get anything back. Then your reward will be great . . . because he is kind to the ungrateful and wicked. Be merciful, just as your Father is merciful. (Luke 6:32-36, NIV)

In the gospels we see Jesus living out his teachings and caring for all kinds of people—a servant of the occupation army, a prostitute, a leper, a person who is possessed. Every time we turn around, we see Jesus restoring sight to the blind, feeding the hungry, preaching good news to the poor. From Genesis to Revelation we are shown a God who demonstrates preferential care for the poor, for the strangers, for those at society's fringes.

Above all else, then, the story of God is a tale of sharing. The God we serve cares for everyone, particularly the powerless ones. And because God cares, God's love is shared through the servant life of God's Son, Jesus Christ. On the cross the Creator even shared our suffering and pain. And in the resurrection God gave birth to a new community of compassion instituted as God's agency for sharing the good news that God's loving kingdom had broken into the world.

The Joy of Sharing

I am a Christmas person. I love Christmas and all it represents. The older I get, the more deeply I appreciate this season in which we celebrate God's extension of remarkable love into our troubled world through the wonder of incarnation.

But the year I was sixteen, Christmastime was the pits. Try as I might, for the first time in my life I couldn't get into the spirit of the season.

I had gotten a job at a Christmas tree lot near my home in San Mateo so I would have money to buy gifts for my family.

But that Christmas tree lot turned into a laboratory study of greed and corruption.

Because my employer, Anthony, had been less than forthright in paying all his taxes in years past, the Internal Revenue Service had stationed a full-time agent at the lot to monitor receipts. But whenever the agent's back was turned, Anthony would sell a tree and pocket the cash.

The other sales staff saw what was going on and followed Anthony's example. Virtually everyone was stealing everyone else blind. I was depressed. I didn't want to be around these people, but it was too late to get another job.

Then I ran into my friend Lou Janakos. Lou saw me moping in the hall at San Mateo High and asked, "What's happening?"

I told him my morbid tale. Lou responded that he knew a new student named Chick Gomes who was really facing the all-time bleakest Christmas of his life. His family had just come from Chicago, and his dad hadn't been able to find work in San Mateo. The family had used all their money in the move and had nothing left for gifts, tree, food—nothing.

I had been aware that some people went without Christmas, but I had never personally known anyone in that spot. My attention shifted from my own depression to the situation facing Chick's family. I wanted to do something but didn't know what.

Then as I was riding my Schwinn to my final day's employment at the Christmas tree lot, I remembered I would get a free tree—and I knew exactly what to do with it! I picked out the biggest, best-shaped tree I could find. At the end of the day I picked up my pay, wished Anthony a merry Christmas, and somehow tied that huge bushy fir on my bike. I struggled down the street looking like a forest on parade.

It took me about an hour and a half to pedal with full foliage to Chick's house in Shoreview—about ten miles from the lot. No one was home, so I put the tree up on the porch and rode off. I felt much lighter biking home and had a good Christmas after all.

The next week I ran into Lou again. "Guess what?" he said. "Somebody gave Chick and his family a Christmas tree, and that was all they needed to get their spirits up. They tied ribbons and strung popcorn over it. They didn't have any gifts, but they still had Christmas."

That completely erased any lingering depression I was feeling. I hadn't had much experience before with sharing outside of my family. But now I had discovered how gratifying it could be to make a little difference for someone else.

God has built us for sharing, and we are most fully ourselves when sharing life with someone else. Sharing is at the heart of a more satisfying way of life. It is also at the center of our corporate life in the church.

More recently I stood in a circle in a small rural village in Haiti. At the end of a three-day planning session for development in the area, we were singing in Creole and English, "We are one in the Spirit. We are one in the Lord."

And we *were* one in the Spirit and in the Lord. As I stood there holding hands with my Haitian brothers, I was almost overcome with emotion. I realized what we had planned in those three days could influence the lives of ten thousand people for the kingdom of God. Though I was only a liaison from World Concern (a Christian development organization) and had little to do with either planning or implementation, I was grateful to God for this opportunity.

That project in Haiti's Plaisance Valley is now complete. A rural health care system is in. People have learned to increase agricultural production, dig wells, and generally better the quality of life in the valley. Since World Concern pulled out, the community has started a cooperative economic development effort using its own resources. And the witness of the church has been significantly strengthened by these programs.

There are so many examples of both individuals and local congregations finding ways to share life. For whatever reason, God has chosen to carry out the loving purposes of the kingdom not only through the Messiah, Jesus, but through a community of people. God instituted the church as God's primary instrument for loving the world.

God intends the church to work for God's compassionate purposes. In the great commandment Jesus instructed us not only to love God with our whole hearts but also to love our neighbors as ourselves. And in the great commission Jesus told us to go into all the world and make disciples of all nations. In those two statements Jesus summarized the mission of sharing God's love through the church. We are to share life with one another as the people of God, then reach out to meet the spiritual and physical needs of a hurting world.

But unfortunately (and as we have seen) while the needs and challenges of the larger society are escalating, North American churches have tended to become more ingrown, more self-serving, more committed simply to maintaining the status quo. To genuinely be the people of God in this generation, we need to reevaluate our priorities and move the mission purposes of God back to the center of our life together. We must set aside all lesser agendas to make God's purposes our own.

In this chapter, then, we will explore reasons an outward focus is often missing from congregational life. We will also explore practical ways we can work with others in our churches to 1. anticipate more effectively the growing challenges that face our world; 2. recover a biblical vision for mission; and 3. create imaginative new ways to act out God's loving purposes in response to the anticipated challenges of tomorrow's world.

Looking Unto the Fields . . .
Today and Tomorrow

Anticipating Global and National Challenges

To move mission back to the center of church life, we need to get in touch with the world around us. We must make an effort to understand our neighborhoods, communities, and the larger society more fully. And we must particularly take time to anticipate the change that is filling our world and identify opportunities for the church to respond.[1]

Most denominations, Christian organizations, and local congregations do long-range planning. The irony and the tragedy is that we plan as though the future is simply going to be more of the present. Anyone who has survived the past few decades should know better. And the rate of change seems to be increasing. But unlike the corporate sector, which spends a great deal of time and money anticipating where new opportunities and challenges are likely to surface, it's the unusual Christian organization that makes an effort to take the future seriously.

In an age of dramatic change, it is essential that the church learn to anticipate tomorrow's challenges. If we can anticipate even a few of the problems coming down the tracks at us, we will have lead time to create compassionate new responses. We will have opportunity to be *proactive* instead of *reactive*.

One way this can work at the local church level is to simply ask who is moving into the community and what are the needs these newcomers bring. For example, Brentwood Presbyterian Church in Los Angeles expects to see a rapid increase in the number of single-parent families in their community. What are the special needs of such a population? Child care, emotional and economic support.

Looking Beyond Ourselves

As we race towards the twenty-first century the church will not even keep pace with tomorrow's challenges unless we radically alter our priorities and the ways we use resources in our individual lives and institutions. This brings us back to the importance of whole-life stewardship and the importance of sharing. We need entire congregations committed to whole-life stewardship.

Someone has facetiously developed a flyer for something called the American Foster Parent Plan. The brochure reads "Poor Nations: Adopt an American! For only $26,000 a year you can adopt an American child and provide the basic necessities of life—television, roller blades and twinkies. For years you third world countries have subsidized American gluttony. Now you can be specific and choose your individual American child and know him by name!"

In the churches I work with in the U.S. and Canada typically at least 80 percent of their time and money never leaves the building. Average giving is 2.8 percent a year by church member, and a very small percentage of that is invested in mission.

We can't begin to respond to the escalating challenges of tomorrows world with this extremely limited investment in mission.

In the concluding days of his life, Dietrich Bonhoeffer wrote, "The church is only the church when it exists for others. The church must share in the secular problems of ordinary human life—not dominating, but helping and serving. It must tell men of every calling what it means to *live in Christ*, to exist for others."[2] I encourage every church to do an annual audit of how much of their time and money actually gets out of the building. If we aren't churches for others are we really churches of Christ at all?

Recovering a Biblical Vision

A Crisis of Vision

Why has the North American church apparently lost its interest in mission at a time when the challenges are escalating so dramatically? Why do we appear so indifferent to the world in which the Creator God has placed us and to God's loving purposes for that world?

One major reason mission gets shoved to the back burner is that our churches are experiencing a crisis of vision. Too few congregations are captured by a vision of what God is doing to make our world new. People don't seem to comprehend the story of God or understand the scope of the Creator God's redemptive purposes. The Bible is right: "Without a vision the people perish." Unfortunately not only are we perishing, those we are called to serve are perishing too.

In the absence of a compelling biblical vision, many of our local congregations seem afflicted by what I call "chronic randomness." The men's group is going one direction, the women's in another, and the young people in a third. Then we have a potluck once a year to congratulate one another that we are still doing the things we did the year before. But nobody knows how it all fits together, because there is no integrating biblical vision.

The closest thing to overarching purpose in most congregations is the unstated goal of "cultural maintenance." Many churches seem to see themselves primarily as cultural mainte- nance stations for providing cultural environments to raise kids as Presbyterian, Mennonite, or Assembly of God. The primary commitment isn't to the radical kingdom vision of changing so- ciety but rather to maintaining the cultural status quo at all costs. And the last thing we expect is that the neighborhoods in which such churches are located will be changed because they are there. These churches don't expect change, don't work for it, and if anything actually happened it would knock their socks off.

A Vision for Whole-Life Mission

To discover God's vision for mission, we must go back to the story of God and try to understand afresh how the Creator God responded to the human condition. In the Old Testament narra- tive, God is concerned about every aspect of the lives of the children of Israel—not just their piety. Of course God wanted the people of Israel to turn from idols to serve and worship the living God. But God also laid down codes for diet. Yahweh mandated economic programs to promote justice for the poor. And Yahweh ordered the people of God to care for widows and orphans and welcome strangers into their midst.

In the life and ministry of Jesus it is impossible to draw a line between the life lived in love, the words spoken in love, and the deeds acted out in love. Jesus' life was a seamless garment of God's love. And we are called to be the living body of Christ in society with the same agenda Jesus had—whole-life mission for the kingdom of God.

Historically, the church in its many traditions has under- stood that we are called both to proclaim *and* to demonstrate the good news of the inbreaking of God's kingdom. But over the last century, too many Christians have understood the mission of the church almost entirely in terms of evangelism, church planting, and discipling.

In the past, especially perhaps in nineteenth-century Britain, evangelical Christians had an outstanding record of social action. In this century, however, partly because of our reaction against the "social gospel" of liberal optimism, we tended to divorce evangelism from social concern, and to concentrate almost exclusively on the former.[3]

During recent decades, Christians from many different traditions have been holding conferences on the nature and mission of the church. International conferences such as Lausanne 74 and the Consultation on the Relationship between Evangelism and Social Responsibility (CRESR 82) have attempted to clarify a biblical view of mission and help us reach a balanced understanding of our Christian responsibility to those in need. Under John Stott's leadership, evangelical theologians concluded at CRESR 82 that "evangelism and social responsibility are like two wings of a bird or two halves of scissors"[4]—neither is fully operational without the other.

When the Wheaton 83 conference was convened at Wheaton College by World Evangelical Fellowship, a group of participants was assigned to study an evangelical understanding of Christian responsibility to a world in need. Over a hundred participants, half from the third world, hammered out a statement, which says in part,

> Some who are inspired by a utopian vision seem to suggest that God's kingdom, in all its fullness, can be built on earth. We do not subscribe to this view since Scripture informs us of the reality and pervasiveness of both personal and societal sin. . . .
>
> Other Christians are tempted to turn their eyes away from this world and fix them so exclusively on the return of Christ that their involvement in the here and now is paralyzed. We do not endorse this view either, since it denies the biblical injunctions to defend the cause of the weak, maintain the rights of the poor and oppressed (Psalm 82:3), and practice justice and love (Micah 6:8). . . .
>
> We affirm that the kingdom of God is both present and future, both societal and individual, both physical and spiritual.[5]

The Wheaton 83 statement worked to avoid the pitfalls of either left or right. Unlike many liberal viewpoints, it recognized that salvation is not the same thing as humanization. Simply helping people become "more fully human" is not saving them. But Wheaton 83 also reached for a more comprehensive statement of mission than some conservatives might endorse, stating that the mission of the church is to speak to the totality of human experience, not just the private spiritual dimension.

The exciting thing is that evangelicals aren't the only Christians coming to such a biblical understanding of mission. Recent reports on world evangelization from the World Council of Churches contain many of the same points of emphasis as the Wheaton statement. And various groups, including Reformed, Anabaptist, and Catholic are developing a kingdom of God theology which transcends the highly politicized theologies of the religious right and left.

The Purposes of God and the Mission of the Church

I propose a definition of Christian mission that reflects the growing understanding of Christians all over the world and avoids either confusing salvation with humanization or limiting God's agenda to the spiritual dimension. Christian mission is *working in partnership with God to see God's comprehensive purposes realized in our lives, in the church—and, in response to the urgent human challenges throughout the world, anticipating the day when Christ returns and the reign of God is established in its fullness.*

In other words, mission means laboring to establish God's reign in the lives of all—while realizing that only at the return of Christ will "every knee bow and tongue confess" his lordship.

Doesn't this way of looking at mission bring it all together in an integrated biblical vision? When we think in terms of laboring with God to see God's reign established everywhere, doesn't the concept of Christian mission become clearer and more compelling? Mission is now something we do not only abroad but also at home.

A New Way Up for the Church

What does this way of looking at mission mean for churches and Christian organizations? Simply that God's purposes must become ours. Even as individual disciples of Jesus must place his purposes at the center of their lives, so must the community of Jesus—the church. In other words, every congregation and Christian organization needs to discern ways to advance the purposes of God. How? Here is one possible format.

1. Study Scripture together, seeking to discern (as in chapter 3) God's loving purposes for God's people and world.
2. Discern through group and individual prayer and active listening specific ways your church or organization is called to work for God's purposes in your community.
3. Listen to the vision God is already placing in your group. This involves not only listening to the leadership but also hearing the story God is planting in every member.
4. As the vision for a congregation or organization comes into sharper focus, orchestrate all the group's time and resources around it. Discontinue dying programs and start new ministries that focus more outwardly on mission.

If we follow this format, we can discover God's vision both for our individual lives and our congregations. Mission will move back to the center of our common life and a growing share of our time and resources will be focused outward. We will become churches for others. And instead of seeking to maintain the present order, by the power of God's Spirit we will help turn the world upside-down.

Wayne Bragg, a consultant in international mission, has vividly pictured God's vision of restoration and reconciliation in a contemporary version of Isaiah's view of the future—written specifically to his Christian sisters and brothers in Kenya. Picture, as you read, God's loving intentions for all people, including your own church and community.

For I create the land of Kenya to be a delight, and her people a joy—
Luo,
 Maasai,
 Kikuyu
 Turkana,
  Kalenjin.

I will take delight in my people, and weeping and cries for help from oppressors shall never again be heard in the land.

There, no child shall ever again die an infant, nor lack food or health care.

No old man shall fail to live out his life; every boy and girl shall live his and her hundred years before dying, and will live out the years in respect and love with the family.

Men shall build houses and inhabit them, plant vineyards and eat their fruit, plant millet, ground nuts, maize and sorghum and eat thereof.

They shall not build for others to inhabit, nor plant to export for others to eat; justice shall ring in the land.

My chosen shall enjoy the fruit of their labor and leisure of their efforts; they shall not toil in vain nor work for absentee landlords.

They care for the land I gave them, it blooms under their tender care.

They shall rule themselves and share in the decision for the people as they see their own needs; nor outsider shall impose his will or plans on them.

Yet nation shall learn from nation, and tribe from tribe; none shall exalt itself over the other.

They shall not toil in vain nor raise children for misfortune, for they are the offspring of the blessed of the Lord, and their children after them.

Before they called to me I will answer, and while they are still speaking I will listen, for they are my people.

Their hearts are attentive to my precepts, they find delight in my laws. My people hear the cries of the needy. They release the yoke of the oppressed.

The man I care for is a man downtrodden and distressed, one who reveres my words.

I will send peace flowing over Kenya like a river, and the wealth of nations over her like a stream in flood.

The Lord shall make his power known among his servants, for see, the Lord is coming in fire with his chariots like a whirlwind, The Lord will judge by fire, with fire he will test all living men.

I myself will come to gather all nations and races, and they shall come and see my glory.

For, as the new heavens and the new earth which I am making shall endure in my sight, says the Lord, so shall your race, and your name endure, and week by week on the Sabbath, all mankind shall come to bow down before me, says the Lord.[6]

Now that vision is large enough to embrace the hopes and longings of all people. Our mission is to become collaborators in God's loving initiative for all peoples. We are invited to become God's agents, empowered by the Holy Spirit to bring people to faith in Jesus Christ and see righteousness established on earth.

We are to bring wholeness to those who are physically, emotionally, and mentally disabled. We are reminded that as a kingdom people we are to work for the restoration and stewardship of God's good creation. We are commended to see the celebrative reign of God established in every dimension of our lives, churches, and society by the power of the Spirit of God.

Acting Out the Compassionate Purposes of God

What are ways this broader vision for the mission of God's kingdom is finding expression in the world around us today? Let's look at congregations that have developed their vision and moved mission to the very center of their common life. Note the broad range of ways God is using them to share life with those around them—actually changing their communities. These congregations can become models for all of us of ways to put God's purposes first by giving top priority to whole-life mission.

Sharing Life in East London

Many people have heard of expensive megachurches in the U.S. Let me share another alternative. Icthus Fellowship in East

London is a remarkable gift to the church. One of the most rapidly growing churches in Europe (over 2,000 members in all), it is made up of a large network of home groups. This burgeoning congregation—made up of West Indians, Pakistanis, working-class British, Asians, and even a few middle-class professionals—tends to contradict the homogeneous principle of some church planters. It is a dynamic model of biblical reconciliation.

Roger Forster, the pastoral leader of Icthus Fellowship, tells me this divergent cross section of East London society is relinquishing long-standing animosities. Despite enormous cultural differences, participants are becoming sisters and brothers in Christ. They are becoming bonded through jubilant worship of the living God, Scripture study, and celebration of the Eucharist. They help one another find work and housing and meet other basic needs. At the same time, they pray for God's Spirit supernaturally to deliver and heal those in need of God's touch.

This church meets in small home groups twice a month and in regional congregational get-togethers once a month. Participants also gather monthly as a fellowship of over a thousand people. Icthus Fellowship is evangelizing and planting new home groups and congregations in East London at a remarkable rate. They are committed to a high level of church growth without using God's money for building programs. They use homes, schools, and existing churches for meetings. People are drawn by the vitality of their faith, the festivity of their worship, the dynamism of their common life, and their commitment to help those in need.

This unusual charismatic church is aggressively involved in evangelism, church planting, discipling, healing, empowering the poor, and working for peace and reconciliation. Over half the time and money of this megachurch for others is invested outwardly in sharing God's love in the world. And they are making a world of difference.

Sharing Life Through Jesus People USA

Over four hundred young people live, share, and minister together as a church and a community on the northside of Chicago. Jesus People USA is both a church and a community in an inner-city area. Eighty members work full time at businesses they own (such as remodeling) so the rest of the community can spend time in ministry.

These young people, many of them new converts, place mission at the center of their church and community life. Their whole-life stewardship involves living with a common purse—all income is shared. That means they can support themselves completely for only $200 per person per month. They live in apartment houses they own. By keeping overhead low, they are able to provide a broad spectrum of ministries to others. Let me mention a few.

Young people in your church may know their band, Resurrection. They also put out a magazine called *Cornerstone*. They feed 250 of their neighbors every day in what they call their Dinner Guest program.

They work at evangelism and discipleship among young drug users on the streets. At the same time, they work with the poor to help them rehabilitate old apartment houses and gain ownership of their own apartments. Their worship services ring with the joy of God.

All of this made possible because Jesus People has decided to live in community with the poor in a tough urban neighborhood. Their witness is having a powerful impact for the kingdom of God—as they orchestrate their entire lives around God's loving purposes.

Sharing Life in the Mathare Valley

Every month thousands of people migrate into the congested Mathare Valley outside of Nairobi. Cardboard boxes, shanties, and open sewers are home to over one hundred thousand refugees in an area three kilometers long and one kilometer wide. Predictably, this brutalizing environment spawns high levels of crime, drug addiction, alcoholism, and prostitution.

Pastor Arthur Kitonga realized that helping the story of God take root in this troubled soil would require more than preaching the good news; it would require a compassionate demonstration of God's caring love as well. In 1974, he and a small community of seven dedicated laymen answered God's call to evangelize the Mathare Valley. Out of their efforts the Redeemed Gospel Church was born, ministering to the full-range of human needs in the valley.

This rapidly growing Pentecostal church now has 1,600 members and over 100 worship centers throughout Kenya. The church sends out teams to conduct two evangelism crusades monthly. This often results in planting new congregations that also minister wholistically in the villages in which they are located.

Slowly the Mathare Valley slums are being transformed by this shalom community God has planted in their midst. The people of Redeemed Gospel Church have concentrated their caring response on the special needs of families with children. For example, they provide nutritional and feeding programs for young children in order to combat malnutrition. They provide health education to increase the level of health and sanitation throughout the entire community.

World Concern recently stumbled upon this remarkable ministry. Committed to empowering the church to enable the poor to become self-reliant, World Concern funded a job-training program the church had initiated. Here, instead of working alongside the church, World Concern is working through the church. Ninety students are being taught carpentry, leatherworking, and sewing to provide them with marketable job skills and reduce the high unemployment in the valley. Kitonga thanks North American Christians "for helping us to hold up the banner of Christ."[7]

Sharing Life in a Hispanic Community

Manuel Ortiz, pastor of Spirit and Truth Fellowship, an independent Hispanic church in Chicago, declares, "We believe that the gospel extends not only to individuals but also to the systemic sin that exists in society. We've given the community an alternative—the kingdom of God."[8]

And indeed they are. They've started Humboldt Christian

School, which offers a Christian education to over two hundred children in the inner city. They operate a thrift store, a family counseling center, and a legal counseling center. Manuel Ortiz is an agent for reconciliation between gangs, such as the Latin Kings and the Spanish Cobras.

No one has to teach poor people about the problems of social justice. The church periodically rallies and marches on city hall or takes some other action to promote justice for the neighborhood.

Two years ago, Spirit and Truth Fellowship divided into four separate groups meeting in homes. "Each house church is developing its own strategy for evangelism and discipleship. One house church has already doubled in size: another plans to send a missionary to Puerto Rico next year."[9]

Manny Ortiz is right. Our task as the people of God is not just meeting urgent human needs, important as that is. Nor is our task simply bringing individuals to faith, critical as that is. We are called to see an entire community live under the reign of God. We are not only called to be the shalom community of God, but to see the purposes of God begin to transform the fabric of life in an entire neighborhood.

Sharing Life in Washington, D.C.

It's in community that we most clearly discover how our lives can be part of God's great drama. Members of Church of the Saviour in Washington, D.C., do a particularly good job of listening to God's call on their lives—collectively and personally. No Sunday-go-to-meeting Christianity for these folks; following Jesus is a whole-life proposition.

Years ago, this congregation felt God was encouraging them to break their one church of some one hundred and twenty members into seven smaller churches. These people have no interest in simply maintaining a certain kind of culture for themselves and their kids. They believe God calls them to make a difference—and they do.

Each of the seven congregations has a specific mission focus—a "calling." For example, there is the Potter's House

Church, whose calling "begins within the Potter's House, a restaurant and bookstore in a poorer part of D.C., which offers hospitality, service, and a listening ear to all who come through its doors."

But Potter's House hospitality also includes running a health clinic next door for those in need. Over thirty-five thousand people a year, many of them Central American refugees, are served. Almost half the staff consists of people from the congregation who donate time on a regular basis out of a shared sense of vocation.

Gordon Cosby, pastor of Church of the Saviour, reminds us,

> The teaching of St. Paul is clear (1 Corinthians 12:1-31 . . .). Each person confessing Christ as Lord, living within the body of Christ, is given a gift by the Holy Spirit for the upbuilding of the Body. We can even say that the person himself, as his essence unfolds under the power of the Spirit, is a gift. He becomes more fully human, more fully Christian. If every member has discovered the unique treasure of his or her own being and is being received by others, there is tremendous fulfillment and power.[10]

Becoming a member of a church such as this demands more than putting a name on a membership roster. To become a member at Church of the Saviour one has to commit to 1. attend worship weekly, 2. participate in a weekly mission support and prayer group, 3. spend time every week in ministry to those in the neighborhood, 4. give a graduated tithe of ten percent and up, and 5. spend an hour a day in prayer. Participants tell me that thousands aren't joining—but when members *are* added, there's a time of real celebration.

Church of the Saviour is having a greater impact than churches many times its size because members have placed mission at the center of their common life. Through small groups they have found a nonbureaucratic way to advance God's loving purposes.

Sharing Life Through Ministries of Reconciliation

The stories of congregations involved in whole-life mission

could go on. All over the world, God's people are preaching good news to the poor, release to the captives, and recovery of sight to the blind. Let me share a few more snapshots of what whole-life mission looks like in today's world.

Recently messianic Jews being persecuted in Israel for their faith in Jesus were rescued and protected by Arab Christians living in Palestine. George Fox College has established an Institute for Peace to search for nonlethal ways to resolve international conflict and educate Christians in the ministry of reconciliation. And Mennonites have established programs to take up where the criminal justice system leaves off—bringing together victims and offenders to promote restitution, reconciliation, and restoration for all parties.

A group of charismatic Catholics works with the poor who live near a garbage dump in Juarez, Texas. This group has believed God for all kinds of miracles. After Christmas, the group prayed for a little girl whose foot and hand had been paralyzed from birth. God healed her, and she has learned to run and play with other kids.[11]

A Southern Baptist church in Houston has started a ministry among AIDS victims. Though this mission was not started as an evangelistic outreach, numbers of the dying have given their lives to God—and have discovered new life in Christ.

One story from Ireland gives particularly compelling evidence of the radical change that takes place when people come to live under the reign of God.

"Had I seen Jimmy on the street before I became a Christian, I wouldn't have hesitated to shoot him. Now he's my brother in Christ, and I would die for him," confessed Liam, a Catholic, age twenty-six, imprisoned for Irish Republican Army terrorist activities. While in prison he participated in a series of IRA prison strikes which culminated in the 1981 hunger strikes which claimed the lives of ten IRA inmates.

After 55 days on the hunger strike and in a coma, Liam was hours away from becoming the eleventh prisoner to die when his mother ordered that he be fed intravenously. While recuperating from the strike, he renewed a former interest in Christianity and started reading the Bible. Understanding he "cannot serve two masters," he realized he had to choose between the IRA political cause and Christ. He chose Christ.

Soon after becoming a Christian, Liam took the brave step of leaving the Catholic tables and walking over to eat with Protestant inmates. He felt the love of God demanded this. He met Jimmy, a Protestant loyalist, and sympathizer with the Ulster Defense League cause. Jimmy and Liam began studying the Bible together with other Christian prisoners, and Jimmy committed his life to Christ. Jimmy and Liam are reconciled in Christ.[12]

Prison Fellowship, which influenced Liam to follow Christ, is committed to reconciling the imprisoned not only to God but to one another. In fact, their understanding of the mandate of the kingdom also motivates them to work actively for structural reform of criminal justice systems all over the world.

We are invited to join thousands of Christians all over the world in working for the comprehensive purposes of God.

Sharing Life and Enjoying the Consequences

The spirit of sharing is the spirit of Christmas. And at least once a year we all learn the tremendous joy that comes from sharing life with others. And sometimes we are surprised at how God uses our sharing to make a difference.

You could smell the savory turkey as soon as you opened the front door of David and Willow Teeter's home in Palestine. The huge turkey in the middle of the long buffet table was surrounded by salads, oranges, a mountain of rice, and plates of Christmas cookies.

This home had become not only a gathering place for a small cluster of Arab Christians but also a "friendship center" where Muslim students dropped in from a nearby university. Surprisingly, the Muslim young people were particularly attracted to this Christian home at Christmastime. Every year they came by the dozens to participate in a Christmas feast that lasts seven days. One year the Teeters served over one hundred sixty full meals plus snacks to their guests.

Each young person was encouraged to bring an ornament

and come early to help decorate the tree. As they decorated the tree, Willow taught them the carol, "Joy to the World." After all the decorating and singing, they plugged in the lights. One Muslim student, a bedouin from the Gaza strip, suddenly exclaimed, "Jesus the light of the world! Jesus the light of the world!" And he quoted several other verses.

The Teeters were astonished. They asked where he had learned these verses.

"From your library," he replied. He had been using their home as a study center.

By Christmas Day, the feast was nearly over and everyone had left. The small community of Christians began to celebrate Christmas by themselves with candles, songs, and prayers. In the middle of their Christmas sing-along, a knock came at the door. There stood some twenty Muslim young men. They were invited in and listened as the Christians continued singing.

The next evening the same group of students came trooping in. The first thing they did was light the candles. They turned off the overhead lights, as had been done the previous evening. Then they said, "Tell us about Jesus. Start at the beginning." The conversations went on into the small hours of the morning.

Perhaps God's story is reflected most compellingly and convincingly in our celebrations, play, and festivity. Remember, Jesus' ministry began at a wedding feast, and his story will conclude in a wedding banquet joyful beyond imagining.

How to Move Whole-Life Mission to the Center of Your Church

As we seek to draw our friends and congregations into a way of life in which mission and sharing are at the center of our life together, where do we begin? Let me outline steps you might try to nudge your church toward whole-life mission.

1. Find a few other people in your church who share your vision for comprehensive biblical mission and prayerfully commit your common vision to paper.
2. Locate modest ways to begin living out your vision in company with those who share your concerns.

3. Meet with key people in leadership in your church. Ask them to share their vision for mission. Then you and your colleagues share yours. Such dialogue can help move mission much more to the center of congregational life—particularly if you offer to help make the vision become a reality.
4. Encourage congregational leaders to—
   a. Identify the specific spiritual and physical needs in your neighborhood today, and anticipate likely needs over the next five years.
   b. Through Bible study and prayer, try to discern God's vision for your congregation.
   c. Audit as accurately as you can how much congregational time and money is presently being spent on yourselves, and how much is being invested in mission to those outside your congregation. Carefully evaluate all proposed building and expansion programs against the mission needs of the international body of Christ.
   d. Set a five-year goal to increase congregational investment of time and money in mission toward 50 percent if possible. (A Presbyterian church in Wabash, Washington, has set and reached this goal!) If your congregation decides to go ahead with a construction project, set a goal of matching every dollar used in construction with a dollar for mission.
   e. Inventory underused resources of time, building facilities, and financial resources in your congregation that could be more fully used in mission.
   f. Create imaginative new forms of mission strategies to use congregational resources more effectively to implement mission vision and meet anticipated human needs in your immediate community and throughout the world.
5. Encourage the development of curriculum for all ages to help members learn to take mission seriously and become world Christians. Donald B. Kraybill's *The Upside-Down Kingdom* and John R. Stott's *Involvement* are particularly good resources for adult study groups.[13]
6. Initiate a program of congregation-wide prayer for renewal through the Spirit of God and for the meeting of spiritual,

physical, and relational needs in your neighborhood and throughout the world.

> And the Conspirator God filled both hands with seed which Jesus spread over Palestine like a lunatic farmer, giving the road and rock an equal chance with the fertile field to go white with harvest. God was taking root. The seed of God grew in secret and went the way of wheat into the blood and sinew of unsuspecting people.[14]

Through whole-life disciples the Conspirator God is changing the world with celebration and great joy. I encourage you and your church to join them by placing God's extended love at the center of congregational life and discovering a new way up.

FOR THOUGHT AND DISCUSSION

Here are three questions to reflect on as you think about becoming more involved in a life of sharing and mission:

1. How is the community around your church likely to change in the next five years? What are likely to be new challenges?
2. What are specific ways your church is seeking to advance the mission purposes of God? How could these purposes of whole-life mission be given greater priority in allocation of congregational time and resources? How could they be moved to the center of the congregational life?
3. What are creative new ways your congregation could respond to anticipated needs and implement God's loving purposes? Ask yourself how God might use you to expand your church's involvement in whole-life mission.

LIFE LINKS

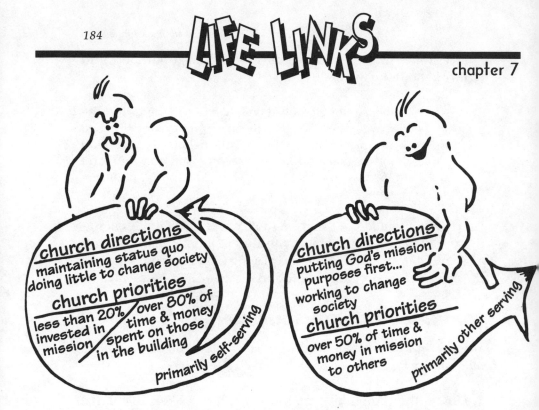

church directions
maintaining status quo
doing little to change society

church priorities
less than 20% over 80% of
invested in / time & money
mission / spent on those
in the building

primarily self-serving

church directions
putting God's mission
purposes first...
working to change
society

church priorities
over 50% of time &
money in mission
to others

primarily other serving

Traditional Approach	Whole-Life Mission Approach
Many of our churches have no clear direction. So they simply settle for maintaining a certain environment for their kids. Their commitment is to maintain the institutional church and the cultural status quo. They don't expect anything to be changed in their community because of them. Change, if it did happen, would knock their socks off! They don't work for kingdom change; their time and money is invested almost exclusively in facilities and programs that will benefit them and their families. Typically, no more than 20 percent of the members' time and money is invested in programs or ministries that touch those outside the building. God's purposes are largely ignored.	Then there are the churches—unfortunately, a minority—which take seriously God's call for the church to be an agent of kingdom change. They place the mission purposes of God—working for righteousness, justice, and peace—at the center of congregational life. They aren't maintaining anything; they are out to see the world changed by the power of God's Spirit. They challenge the secular values of materialistic culture at every turn. Typically their commitment to kingdom change is reflected in new congregational priorities—even to the point of investing at least 50 percent of time and resources in ministering to others! These churches make a difference.

8

Creating New Possibilities

reating! The Story of God begins with creation—with the spectacular, extravagant creativity of God. Before anything existed, the Creator God was; out of nothing God created everything.

Our Creator has graciously gifted us, as the divine image bearers, with creativity. Though we are not able, like God, to create something from nothing, we are able to imagine and bring into being a lavish array of new possibilities for ourselves and God's world. Most important, we are invited, as God's children, to join the Creator in the task of re-creation—for the Bible makes it clear that God intends to make all things new.

Of course, when we place God and God's story at the center of our lives, God begins re-creating us. And God gives the creative opportunity to fashion our entire lives around God's purposes. But the Creator God also gives us the remarkable creative opportunity to join God in seeing this world changed, too. That's what this chapter is about enabling you to create new possibilities for your life and God's world. . . . Creating a way of life you can truly love!

We will explore 1. the meaning of creativity and the need for it in the Christian community; 2. common barriers to creativity and how to overcome them; 3. specific methods for creating new possibilities for our lives in the drama of God; and 4. examples of those who have found innovative ways to collaborate with the Creator God.

Creativity—an Untapped Resource

I conduct futures/creativity workshops with Christian organizations and churches all over the United States, Canada, and many other countries. I have come to believe that creativity is a great untapped resources in the church today. I have seen remarkable things happen when people learn to unleash their imaginations to create new possibilities for God's kingdom.

I cannot think of the word *creative* without remembering one bright sunny day in Estes Park, Colorado, where I conducted a daylong creativity session with the Sisters of Mercy. As part of the workshop, the Sisters divided into groups to work on a "creativity task." Before they started, I challenged them to jettison conventional approaches to living out faith and solving problems. I urged them to be creative, divergent, and "seriously weird." They didn't disappoint me.

After two hours, the creativity groups streamed back into the lodge. As the first group got up to share, I saw a twinkle in their eyes. Their creativity task had been "to create an imaginative new approach to justice, education, and helping the poor."

I asked, "What do you have for us?"

"The Traveling Solar Circus and the Mercy Clowns!"

"What in the world is that?" I asked.

"We plan to construct a circus tent with panels of all different colors. Then we will put solar collectors on the outside to run everything inside the tent. We'll set up our multicolored tent in a small Honduran village. We'll dress like clowns, then through puppetry, mime, and dramatics we'll teach the people of the village about literacy, sanitation, and community health.

"But that's not all. During offseason we'll take our tent— solar collectors and all—to an affluent suburban shopping center in Southern California. There the Sisters of Mercy clowns will teach the upwardly mobile about social justice, the poor, and whole-life stewardship."

Now that's creative! That's the level of imagination we must have to burst out the old wineskins of convention and create new and more effective ways to implement the vision of God in our lives and our world.

Defining Creativity

What do I mean when I speak of creativity? *Working in partnership with the Creator God to generate new possibilities.*

This definition is important, because it is crucial that we recognize where our creativity comes from—our Creator, whose sheer inventiveness and imagination is astonishing.

> . . . God thinking up a giraffe, a cucumber, the overtone series, sexual reproduction, gravity, dolphins and strawberries. He is none of these and there were none of these for him to copy. There was simply no information that he could gather outside of his own imagination that would give him an inkling of what to make and how to make it.[1]

Because creativity originates with the Creator God, a positive use of imagination requires acknowledging and working with the Creator. As Emil Brunner says,

> God the Creator, having created man in his image, has given him creative powers; where man acknowledges his Creator, he knows that he cannot create from nothing as God does, that therefore human creativity is a mere imitation of God's. . . .[2]

Brunner points out that if we seek to use our God-given creativity autonomously apart from God, we will face "the gravest consequences." But if we use our imaginations in collaboration with the Creator's imagination, the possibilities for the kingdom are unlimited.

Since we took the first bite of the forbidden fruit in the Garden, we have sought autonomy from God. We thought as we sank our teeth deep in that forbidden fruit that we would know as God knows and be powerful as God is powerful. We thought we could do it our way.

We couldn't have been more mistaken. We have indeed used our God-given creativity in autonomy from the Creator, and we are experiencing the "gravest of consequences." Although some of humankind's new expressions of creativity add to the beauty and bounty of all that God has created, others reflect the darkest side of human nature, threatening both human life and creation itself. We have used our God-given creativity to build a high-tech Babel for which we and those with whom we share the planet are paying a very high price.

Harvey Cox asserts that the human creature,

> While gaining the whole world . . . has been losing his own soul. He has purchased prosperity at the staggering impoverishment of the vital elements of his life. These elements are festivity—the capacity for genuine revelry and joyous celebration, and fantasy—the faculty for envisioning radically alternative life situations.[3]

But we also have the option of using our God-given creativity to be collaborators in the inbreaking of God's kingdom. If we do, we will also discover a renewal of the festive, celebrative, joyful aspects of life that God intended.

Barriers to Creativity

If creativity is so wonderful, why do so many of us in the church seem so bound by convention, so stuck in the same old ways of doing things? There are a number of reasons. Most of us—both as individuals and in groups—have unconsciously erected barriers that block our creativity and stifle our imaginations. To reawaken our imaginations, we must first identify and remove as many barriers as possible.

One important barrier is fear of change. Never has the church more desperately needed new ideas for ways to advance God's kingdom. We need new approaches to ministry, community, lifestyle, and vocation. But at the same time there seems to be an inherent resistance in the church to any type of change. Someone has written that the seven last words of the church are "We've never done it that way before."

Resisting change is a natural human response. But to create with God, we must relinquish our conventional approaches, understandings, and expectations; we must fling open the windows of our lives to new possibilities. While we can all affirm "Christ is the same yesterday, today, and forever," we need to realize that is not necessarily true of our conventional ways of doing things.

How do we reduce fear of change? By taking it slow—trying a little selective change rather than sweeping revolution. By focusing on the benefits of creating new possibilities—and studying firsthand examples of others who changed and benefited from it. By internalizing the reality that only those who do a little selective risk-taking experience what it's like to be fully alive. And of course by spending significant time in prayer.

But resistance to change is not the only barrier to creativity. In many Christian traditions there is a deep distrust of imagination itself. Some of our Christian ancestors, such as the Puritans, saw imagination as the playground of Satan. They encouraged development of the intellect but were suspicious of imagination. Many of us have inherited this attitude. Although we don't consciously think that imagination or creativity are sinful, we tend to discount them as trivial or unimportant.

One has only to examine the relatively small contribution Christians are making in the arts to suspect we still distrust our imaginations. There is too little emphasis in Christian day schools, colleges, and churches on developing the imaginative powers the Creator God has given us.

If we believe God redeems us as whole persons, however, and intends to use us as whole-life disciples, it follows that God intends to use our imaginations and creativity as well as our intellects, powers of communication, and relational gifts.

It's time we embraced the reality that creativity and imagination are wonderful gifts from God. It's time we enjoyed them—and employed them much more fully to advance God's kingdom. We need a renaissance of Christian creativity. We need the Holy Spirit to create a whole generation of innovative dreamers committed to making God's dreams become reality.

But this brings us to another major barrier to creativity—the belief some people have that they aren't creative. People tend to think that imagination and creativity are gifts possessed by a small elite of artists, authors, and musicians.

Nothing could be further from the truth! I've found in over nearly twenty years of doing creativity workshops that *everyone* is gifted with creativity and imagination. Some, of course, have exercised their imaginations more than others—but God has given us all the capability of imagining and creating new possibilities. Those who feel they aren't creative simply need to exercise their "imagination muscles" more.

So even if you think creativity is for others, even if you're skeptical about your creativity and fearful of trying new possibilities, read on. I believe you will find that "the water's fine."

Pathways to Creative Living

I often find much more creativity in the secular society than in the church. For example, when employed in business research at the Weyerhaueser Corporation, I worked with people committed to divergent thinking and creative planning. They gave birth to a range of new corporate ventures—such as fish farming on their forest lands. And years before the energy crisis they used wood waste to heat their facilities.

In Sweden there is even a school for entrepreneurs, called the Foresight Group, established in 1980 to train people to come up with new answers, solutions, and ideas. As a result, a draftsman has started an eel farm in an abandoned section of the plant where he works. It will produce more than one hundred tons of eels annually.

A salesman in Sweden has designed an innovative way to fabricate concrete elevator shafts that can be installed in existing apartments without breaking down walls. There has been tremendous demand for the new product because Sweden, in the interest of handicapped people, has recently passed a law making elevators mandatory in buildings above a certain height.[4] If secular society can come up with ideas like that, Christians can draw on the same innovative powers to create new approaches to vocation, celebration, whole-life steward-ship, and whole-life mission.

But how do people go about creating the new and innova-tive? What are creative methodologies we can use to create with God? Here are three possibilities: 1. "Many trails to you"—Ex-panding your options. 2. Venturing off the beaten path. 3. Cre-ating your own road home.

Many Trails to You—Expanding Your Options

A distressingly large number of Christians limit focus on a depressingly narrow range of life options. College students, for example, often think about vocation in terms of a small range of occupational choices. They limit themselves to a conventional array of timestyles and lifestyles that often have little to do with the kingdom. And the guidance programs in many Christian colleges, as well as the leaders of Christian ministry organiza-tions on secular campuses, do too little to help students explore nontraditional lifestyle, vocation, and ministry options.

But college students aren't the only ones who limit them-selves; most of us get stuck in narrow life ruts. As a result, we live rather conventional, compartmentalized lives. Few have discovered the adventure of significantly broadened options.

The first step in creating new possibilities is to make the mouth of your creativity funnel as wide as possible. First do re-search in your area of interest. Collect as broad an array of ideas as you can think of—even those that seem unlikely.

Roger Von Oech, a noted writer on creativity, helps us think about expanding options by giving many answers to the ques-tion, "How do you keep a fish from smelling?" The possibilities are broader than what you might think: "Cook it as soon as you catch it. Freeze it. Wrap it in paper. Keep a cat around it. Burn incense. Leave it in water. Cut its nose off."[5]

In working with college students interested in serving over-seas, I find many limit themselves to traditional missionary roles. I try to help them expand their range of options to include teaching in nonformal settings, teaching English as a second language, working in community health, training in small-scale technology or tropical agriculture, providing theological education by extension, or taking "tentmaking" occupations overseas (jobs to support oneself financially while working for mission).

Some friends and I are interested in creating a new Celtic Prayer Retreat Center. And I am trying to take the "many trails" approach in looking at the possibilities. On a trip to Europe, for example, I visited Cistercian abbeys, Benedictine monasteries, and Protestant lay communities. In the United States, I intentionally plan my trips so as to visit as many different communities as possible. And of course I read widely. I am discovering many more trails that lead to community than I had imagined.

I realize not everyone can travel overseas. But there are creative models right in your own area. And reading materials on alternatives for Christians are abundant. Turn to your library, bookstore—even your telephone book and newspaper—to seek out new ideas and see what others are doing. Don't exclude anything at this point. Exploring all options will give you more to work with—and pray about. Many trails to you!

Venturing off the Beaten Path

If you're going to be creative, however, it isn't enough simply to expand your options. You'll also need to venture off the beaten pathway. Look for more than obvious answers. Seek out the divergent. Explore wildly unlikely possibilities.

A city in the Netherlands had a trash problem. Garbage was gathering around homes and buildings. The town was an eyesore. The townspeople explored many options—more litter patrols, more garbage cans. But none worked.

So they left the beaten path. In one problem-solving session, someone suggested paying people for putting litter in trash cans. While this idea wasn't economically feasible, it became a springboard for considering some truly divergent alternatives, including the brilliant but offbeat idea which finally worked.

The sanitation department developed electronic trash cans which had a sensing unit on the top which would detect when a piece of refuse had been deposited. This would activate a tape-recorder that would play a recording of a joke. In other words, joke-telling trash cans! Different kinds of trash cans told different kinds of jokes. Some told puns; others told shaggy dog stories, and soon developed reputations. The jokes were changed every two weeks. As a result, people went out of their way to put their trash in trash cans, and the town became clean once again.[6]

Some Polynesian Christian young people living in Hawaii used familiar entertainment vehicles to create a wholly new vocation for the story of God. They started a new group called Island Breeze to entertain at Hawaiian resorts and in doing so found a way off the beaten path.

They put together a program that presents authentic traditional dances from Maroi, Samoan, and Tongan cultures. But they also work Christian songs into their repertoire. Their show is entirely different from any I have seen in Hawaii, and there is no way for the audience to miss their clear Christian witness.

In addition to sharing their music, their culture, and their witness, this innovative group has created a ministry through which they use a generous share of their profits to bring other young Christians from the South Pacific islands to receive Christian education at The University of the Nations in Hawaii, and support Christian mission and activities throughout Asia by working with Youth with a Mission.

Creating Your Own Road Home

Beyond expanding your range of options and venturing off the beaten path, we also have the possibility of creating something almost totally new by "creating our own road home." I am talking about getting "seriously weird" in imagining new possibilities for existing realities—turning what is tried and true on its ear and giving ourselves permission to be a little crazy in dreaming up what could be. Creating something new is especially useful as a spark to the creativity process itself; trying to go where no person has dared to go before can be a big help in breaking free from the barriers to creativity.

Some groups use a creativity process called *synetics* to combine two totally unrelated items or concepts to create something entirely new. For example, what do you think of when you hear the term, "aerosol peanut butter"? Imagine all the possible uses (provided you can get it out of the can)—cake decorating, kid's lunches, catering, dental adhesive, an underarm deodorant. Has your imagination begun to take hold of the creative challenge?

Or look at something ordinary in your life—for example, a seamstress's box of fabric scraps such as Velcro, acrylic trims, and so on. What would happen if you broke loose from seeing these as ordinary materials and looked at them from an entirely new perspective?

Let me share with you a letter to the San Francisco *Chronicle* in which the author did just that. Note the freshness and the fun.

> I find your story in last Monday's *Chronicle* about the invention of Velcro highly unlikely. I have been told by a reputable source that Velcro is derived from the hide of Velcros, distant relatives to the Naugas. But now that Velcro has become such a lucrative commodity, the Velcros are threatened with extinction. The wholesale slaughter of these helpless animals compounds the already difficult situation Velcros face in the wild. They easily stick to things, and during mating become literally stuck on one another and hence are easy prey to hunters.
>
> For a long time Velcros were worshiped by the Acrylics, a primitive tribe of weavers who lived in their habitat. The Acrylics protected the Velcros for religious purposes, but the commercial exploitation of the Acrylics for their weavings, and their subsequent fall from fashion favor, has forced the disintegration of Acrylic society. It is the same old story. We have seen it on every nature program on Channel 9. First come the explorers, then the traders and the missionaries. Finally, the designers and consultants, leading to the complete ruination of a noble people, the destruction of habitats, and the extinction of their denizens.[7]

Some Christians in New Zealand came up with something wonderfully wild and creative that is making a difference. Nelson, New Zealand, like many small cities in the U.S., has a problem. It is a community of 40,000 with nothing for the young people to do on the weekend. As a consequence many teenagers and young adults hang out at local taverns.

A group of Christians concerned about the problem came up with an imaginative new solution to address this crisis. They created an underage night club called the "Led Zebra."

As soon as we step through the door we recognize that we are in a different world. We feel like we are on safari in Africa. As we enter the entertainment area of this unusual night club, we see wall panels giving the impression that elephants are coming toward us on one wall and a pride of lions are relaxing in the savannah on the other. A nine-foot metal zebra standing on its haunches greets us.

Someone hits a switch; the zebra's laser eyes start doing a laser light show on the ceiling. The lights onstage come up as a band enters and begins to perform. Now a full-scale light show, based on state-of-the-art technology, starts up; smoke rises from beneath the walls. Some 400 young people, crowded wall-to-wall in the Led Zebra, clap and move to the music.

The entire amazing show is operated by engineers in one corner in a huge pot (the kind you cook missionaries in). The Led Zebra is packed out every weekend with young people who seem to enjoy this much more than the tavern scene. One other creative twist—Sunday morning the Led Zebra is a new church planted for young people who don't feel comfortable in traditional churches.

Can you give yourself permission to get seriously weird—to imagine something as wild as the Led Zebra to address needs in your community, or create a new Christian cooperative for God's kingdom, or a brand new Christian celebration?

Unleashing Your Imagination

If you have stayed with me all the way through this book, you may be at an important threshold. You may have concluded you can no longer give yourself to the tired tales with which you have been raised or the high stress lifestyles with which you have to contend. You are ready for a change. You are ready to join thousands of others in embracing the story of God.

But as you know changing life direction isn't easy. Any kind of change—not to mention risky new options—is scary business. Yet change and newness can also be liberating. Remember the changes God intends to make in your life are only for the better. Keep moving forward. The destination is worth the journey!

What you and I will find—you may already be discovering it—is that the more we bring our life into alignment with the purposes of God, the more we find ourselves working *with* God's creation, not against it. You see, God only intends good for our lives. The Creator God intends that we discover a way of life not only in which we blossom and grow, but in which we enable others to flourish. Where are the handles? How can we actually begin to create whole new possibilities for our own lives, communities, and churches?

Idea Storming—How to Create a Life You Can Love

Let me outline a creativity processes you can try with your friends called "idea storming." This is a variation on the idea of "brainstorming," which has proved itself over and over again in corporate and institutional settings. I have tried to adapt the standard brainstorming techniques to Christians in search of new possibilities.

In this group process, have over a group of friends, or try this in place of a committee meeting. Do it at home or in another relaxed setting. Serve nachos or other delectables, dress causally, and try to create a relaxed, informal environment.

Develop a specific list of creativity tasks ahead of time and focus on one creativity task at a time. What these are will depend on the nature of your group. If you are a church committee, you might pick one task or challenge facing the committee. If you are a small group studying this book together, you might pick issues raised in earlier sessions. Here are possibilities.

1. How can we create lifestyles and timestyles that are more festive and less stressed?
2. How can we create a more cooperative way of life with others, perhaps including co-op housing?
3. How can we create families for others? (Kids and parents doing ministry together)
4. How, through the arts, can we raise consciousness in our congregation regarding our responsibility for human need?
5. How can we create new ministries that empower for unemployed young people to become self-reliant?
6. How can we create a video production company to reach fringe youth?
7. How can we create a multicultural celebration of God's kingdom?

If your group is large, break into smaller groups and allow people to work on the creativity task that interests them most. Groups should be made up of three to eight people—beyond eight people, groups tend to become unmanageable. Ask someone in each group to keep the group focused on the task.

Phase One—Idea Capture

In the group, read over your creativity task again. Then begin generating ideas. Select a scribe and give him or her several large sheets of newsprint to capture everyone's ideas.

At this point, no one should evaluate the ideas; the purpose is to come up with as many ideas as possible. Group members should be encouraged to be divergent and "seriously outrageous" in the idea-capture phase. Allow about forty-five minutes for this part of the process.

Phase Two—Idea Cluster

After you have captured as many ideas as you can from your group, ask participants to reach consensus on what they feel are the three most compelling ideas. Ask the scribe to circle those ideas. Then explore imaginative ways you might combine the three ideas into a cluster. How could the idea be combined into a working whole?

Next expand the cluster idea, moving into specific goals and strategies for implementing the cluster. Give your new cluster of ideas an imaginative new name that is at least as creative as the ideas you came up with.

If your group storming session involves more than one group, prepare a stimulating three-minute presentation or skit to introduce your ideas to the larger group. Or if yours is the only group involved, decide how you would present your idea to someone else. Allow about twenty minutes.

Phase Three—Idea Communication

If several creativity groups have been involved, assemble all the groups and give each one opportunity to share in three minutes a brief summary of the group storming list and present the top idea cluster. Encourage people to affirm one another and enjoy their creativity as they share their ideas.

Now, whether your groups are large or small, allow time for participants to discuss how they are feeling about their ideas; indicate if they are interested in seeing any of the ideas that were presented actually take life and become a reality; and design a follow-up process to enable those interested in seeing ideas implemented to actually do the necessary research, prayer, and planning. This final phase could take anywhere from thirty to sixty minutes, depending on the number of creativity groups involved.[8]

Creativity for the Kingdom

I guarantee that if you try unleashing your creativity with a group of friends you will have a good time. You may even come up with imaginative new ways to change your own life or even make a difference in the world. Then of course you need to develop ways to implement ideas that are particularly compelling.

Let me share some of the more imaginative approaches I've come across. Some came out of a creativity process like the one

I just described. Others came out of the fertile imaginations of those determined to give creative new expression to the story of God. The first one comes from my own home.

Coming Home to the Kingdom

For my wife, Christine, and me, this business of following Jesus and changing our way of life is not a matter of giving things up. It is instead a wonderful creative adventure. All of life has become a design opportunity. We are constantly looking for imaginative ways to reflect something of the festivity of God's kingdom in every area of our life together.

For example, because the coming of God's kingdom is going to be a wonderful multicultural celebration, we cook a lot of international dishes—stir-fry curries or peasant foods from all over the world. Such meals are more festive, less expensive, and healthier than conventional foods (less meat, fat, and sugar; and more fruits, vegetables, and fiber).

When we entertain we invariably cook international. For example, I fix a complete Haitian meal I learned to cook from my friends in Haiti. Or Christine prepares a delicious Greek meal, doing lovely things with eggplant, mushrooms, and garlic. I believe it really does give us a little foretaste of the celebration of the kingdom. (By the way, Herald Press has an excellent cookbook on international cooking entitled *Extending the Table*.)[9]

Then take the interior design of our homes. I have Christian friends who spent $60,000 to turn their main floor into what looks like an exquisite museum. But you're afraid to touch anything and in no way does their home reveal their faith. Other friends decorate their homes with plastic wall hangings from Penney's and not a lot of taste. The only sense of the sacred is a little wall plaque invoking God's blessing. Some of my radical friends decorate their homes with orange crates and serious levels of ugliness.

Is this all there is? Aren't there other options for creative Christians? Can't we bring the things we believe and value into the interior design of our homes? Can't we design our homes around themes central to our Christian faith, such as Advent,

Jubilee, or the great homecoming of God?

Christine and I are trying to decorate our main floor around the biblical theme of Jerusalem as the great homecoming of God. We don't know precisely how to proceed. But when people come into our home we want them to sense the joy and celebration of God's homecoming, though they may not fully identify the theme. Once we biblically redefine the good life all of life becomes a wonderful creative opportunity.

Creating Random Hospitality

At a creativity workshop at Brentwood Presbyterian in Los Angeles, workshop participants came up with a new way to celebrate hospitality. They are a large suburban congregation where a lot of folks don't know each other, so they found a way to get people connected. People willing to have others over for dinner simply printed up an invitation and randomly placed it beneath a pew somewhere in the sanctuary. During the morning worship the congregation was asked to check beneath the pews. Those who found invitations also found new friends.

Creating Economic Empowerment

Tragically, we in North America are in the process of creating a permanent underclass of tens of thousands of young people who will live and die without having found jobs. And it's not because they are lazy or shiftless. Rather, they have gone to inner-city schools which are not teaching them to read and write. They have no job skills, and there is no place in our economy for illiterate, unskilled people.

Tom Skinner Associates imaginatively responded to this challenge. They rented an empty building across the street from an inner-city high school in Newark, New Jersey. They put computers in the building and are using those computers to teach a small group of high school people basic literacy skills. They are also teaching them to program and service the computers. Those young people are knocking themselves out to get in this program because they know if they successfully complete it, they can break out of the cycle of unemployment.

By the way, do you have any idea what software Skinner Associates has them use to program the computers? That's right—the Scriptures. Numbers of those young people are becoming Christians while developing job skills. We need a whole generation of new ministries that combine witness and empowerment for the kingdom of God.

Creating Christian Scrounging

Going through a creativity session with a group of participants in the SCUPE Urban Conference in Chicago, I asked people to find something thrown away in the city and do something for the kingdom with it.

When the group returned from their session, I wondered, "What do you have?"

They responded, "Old tires thrown away on the streets. We're going to stack them nine tires high and fill the stacks with dirt and potato seeds. We'll water it from the top; the potato sprouts will come out the side. At harvest time we'll push over the tires, pick up the potatoes, and sweep up the dirt."

I said, "You're kidding."

"Nope. It's called vertical gardening, and it will work."

What underused resources could we transform into tools for the kingdom? In the 1990s and beyond, we'll all need to become creative scroungers to get the job done.

Creating Self-support

Dan Schellenberg is a Southern Baptist missionary who has found some marvelously creative ways to transform underused resources in Kenya into evangelism, discipling, and church expansion. He has created a range of imaginative new ways to empower the powerless in rural Kenya.

For example, he enabled pastor Ngozi of Mbembani Church to live self-sufficiently and have more time to spread the gospel and serve his congregation. Together Dan and Pastor Ngozi planned a homestead for the pastor that generated enough income for Pastor Ngozi to become self-supporting.

First they built a water catchment system. Pastor Ngozi not only used the water to irrigate a new garden but was able to sell water to others at a going rate.

Second came a silo to provide grain storage for the excess grain produced through irrigation.

Phase three was a $45 biogas digester which uses cow dung to produce methane gas for lights and energy. All of these steps not only give the pastor's family a buffer against famine but provide regular income from the sale of water, grain, and animals.[10]

Creating Hope for Throwaway Kids

Too many families in Haiti have more kids than they can really afford and must give some children to other families to serve as indentured servants until they are liberated at age eighteen. I interviewed Marie. She was a ten-year-old who had not seen her family since she became a servant child three years earlier.

Marie worked from six in the morning to ten at night, seven days a week. She did all the dirty work and got whatever was left over from the family's meals. Marie had no way to compare her circumstances to children in the U.S., but she was constantly reminded of the difference between her way of life and those of the biological children in the family. The biological children went to school and church; they celebrated birthdays and Christmas. Marie did none of these things.

Chavannes Jeune, president of the Evangelical Baptist Church of Haiti, worked with Christians in the United States to come up with an imaginative response to this tragic situation. They created a literacy and vocational program exclusively for servant children.

Essentially Chavannes talked the employers of these servant children into letting them off two hours every evening to learn reading, math, and personal survival skills. Once they are literate they are trained in a basic vocational skill—such as carpentry, masonry, or sewing—so that when they are liberated at eighteen they can break out of the cycle of poverty.

Through this creative program these children are not only becoming literate and developing job skills, many of them in response to this expression of the love of God are becoming vital Christians. Today thousands of kids in Haiti have hope for the future because some Christians in Haiti and the U.S. cared enough to be creative. (For those who would like to support the work of the church in Haiti write: Chavannes Jeune, President, MEBSH, c/o World Concern, Box 33,000, Seattle, WA 98133)

Called to Be Creative

Within every image bearer of God is the creativity to imagine and create whole new ways to participate in the adventure of God. Don't limit yourself to tired tales and conventional options. Join those who are inviting God's Spirit to blow through their imaginations and give fresh expression to the story of God. Let's live as though we believed it.

Elizabeth O'Connor reminds us that

> in every person is the creation story. Since the first day of our beginning, the Spirit has brooded over the formless, dark void of our lives, calling us into existence through our gifts until they are developed. And that same Spirit gives us the responsibility of investing them with him in the continuing creation of the world. Our gifts are the signs of our commissioning, the conveyors of our transforming creative power.[11]

Let's join thousands all over the world who are discovering the secret of significant living, who are participating with the Spirit of the living God to create not only a life we can love but also is making a world of difference in a world of need . . . in the name of Jesus Christ.

FOR THOUGHT OR DISCUSSION

1. Why do we need to break out of the wineskins of convention and create new approaches to life and mission?
2. What are your barriers to creativity—what in your life tends to hold you back from exploring new possibilities?

3. Try the creativity methods described in this chapter. What new ideas can you come up with to make a difference? How will you begin your creative journey to put God's purposes first in your life, family, congregation community?

Confined to the Conventional	Liberated to Be Creative
Many Christians—and congregations—confine themselves to a narrow range of options as they look toward the future. They stay by the safe shores of the familiar, regardless of whether this strategy brings the desired outcome. Individuals tend to limit ministry, vocational, and lifestyle options to those with which they have been raised. Congregations tend to plan simply to do more of the same—whether it's effective or not. Unwittingly they smother their creativity and confine themselves to a small cubicle due to their fear of exploring beyond the conventional.	But a growing number of Christians are bursting out of the confining conventional boxes with which they have been raised. They are discovering the delight of creating a much broader array of ways to seek first the purposes of God in their lives and congregations. They are creating imaginative new approaches to whole-life discipleship— orchestrating their whole lives around the purposes of God. They are creating new ministries and new celebrations. And they are having the time of their lives. Join them in unleashing your creativity to express the joyful inbreaking of the kingdom of God.

Begin Now

Beginning! Beginning any new initiative requires a deliberate choice. It won't just happen. The easiest thing in the world is simply to go with the flow—avoid choices, risks, new beginning—and live with the consequences and the regrets.

It was once reported on *Good Morning America* that a group of people over ninety-five years of age were asked a single question. "If you could live your life over again, what would you do differently?"

Responses varied, of course. But three answers dominated. If respondents could live their lives over again they would—

- take more time to reflect.
- take more risks.
- do more things that would live on after they died.

They're right, you know. The good life has nothing to do with mindless accumulation and frenetic scrambling. Living on after we die are the things we give away. That's exactly what Christ told us—only in losing life do we find it.

In this book we have argued that if we want our lives to have meaning and purpose, we must abandon the half-truths and full fictions to which we have given ourselves. And we must embrace a new story and become part of a new venture that is quite literally changing the world. . . . A new way up.

Listen again to the compelling power of that story as John Westerhoff remembers it for us.

In the beginning, God had a dream of a world at one with itself; it was the world God intended at creation, a world of peace and unity, of freedom and equality, of justice and well being of all peoples.

We were created in God's image to enjoy God's dream, but with the capacity to say "yes" or "no" to it. And so the plot thickened. We humans didn't turn out as God had hoped. We were more interested in our own dreams than in God's dream. . . .

But God is persistent. Having planted the dream deep within our conscience, God calls forth and raises up witnesses to the lost dream. God made a covenant with us so that forever we will experience the unswerving, patient pull of God toward the dream. God saved us from slavery, led us on a pilgrimage to a promised land, and gave us moral commandments to love God and neighbors so that we might live for God's dream. God raised up leaders to guide us and at last prophets to remind us of our covenant and to sketch a picture of what the world would be like if God's dream were realized.

Still, we frustrated God's dream by acting like all the rest of humanity. It is as if we were in bondage to the social, political, and economic systems we created. So God made a decision. God acted again, came to us in Jesus of Nazareth, the dreamer, storyteller, doer of deeds, healer of hurts, advocate of the outsider, liberator of the oppressed; in Jesus, God shares our common lot and overcomes the principalities and powers that keep us from living the dream.

Good news has been announced. God's dream has begun; God's dream will come. Yet the dawn of hope is not yet the high noon of God's dream come on earth. Darkness still covers much of the earth and we still live as if this were the best of all possible worlds. But a new possibility exists. We have been given a new pair of eyes and with them the vision of dreamers returns.

We have been called into a visionary community to live risky, laughable lives of tomorrow's people, to live in and for God's dream, to witness to a world of peace and unity, of freedom and equality, of justice and well being for all people. We are called to accept the cost and the joy of discipleship, to proclaim in word and deed the good news of God's dream come true. God promises us courage and strength in the struggle for peace and justice; God forgives us our failures and lifts us up to new possibilities; God is present in our trials and rejoicing and hopes from this day forward.[1]

From this day forward we have the opportunity, by the power of God, to begin over—to place God's dream and loving purposes at the very center of our lives. If we do, we will discover a way of life with purpose that makes a difference in the world today—and will have a lasting impact tomorrow. We will truly find a life we can love.

For whatever reason, God has chosen to work through ordinary people like you and me to change the world. And Jesus still stands at the edge of history inviting us to drop our nets, abandon our boats, and join him in the great adventure of seeing all things made new. What an incredible opportunity!

I have attempted in this book to show you creative ways we can all be more a part of God's dream and purposes. Now the ball is in your court. Spend time in prayer as you conclude this book, listening to God, writing down what you hear God saying to you, developing modest first steps. Then find one or two other people determined to put God's kingdom first in their lives; share with them the small initial steps you plan to take. Ask for their prayers to hold you accountable for the changes God is calling you to make.

I am interested in learning how God is drawing others into his kingdom initiative. I would enjoy hearing the ways in which God is calling you. And I am always looking for new creative examples of places where the kingdom is taking root. Drop me a note—Tom Sine, Box 45867, Seattle, WA 98145.

Throughout this book we have emphasized that the Jesus we follow didn't come calling us to a self-interested faith. Quite the contrary. As we follow Jesus through the pages of the New Testament we always find him in one of two places—either with God in extended times of prayer, solitude, and worship, or with people in sharing, healing, and celebrating life. Even as Jesus was a man for others we are called to be a people for others . . .

placing God's purposes first in our lives . . . "Good news to the poor, sight to the blind and release to the captives."

When we determine to be people for others and place God's story and loving purposes at the center of life, all of life becomes a creative opportunity to manifest God's jubilant kingdom. That brings us to the final story—about a couple I know who found an imaginative way to manifest God's kingdom through their wedding celebration.

In a day in which young people (and their parents) often go into serious debt to get married, Terry and Patty created a refreshingly divergent approach. Not only did they keep the costs of the wedding to a minimum, having friends donate flowers and take the pictures, they had a wedding reception those who attended will never forget.

In their wedding announcement, Terry and Patty wrote that they didn't want regular gifts for their wedding. Their note explained, "We have our health, each other, and opportunities to serve the Lord. We simply don't need a lot of things. Instead, we would appreciate it if you gave us turkeys, potatoes, or cranberry sauce." Their bewildered families and friends complied but didn't understand until after the wedding.

Now Patty and Terry work in a number of ministries at University Baptist Church in Seattle, including a Saturday feeding program for the elderly, poor, and street people in the University District. As the homeless street people sauntered into the church basement for their usual meal that particular Saturday, however, they were amazed to find the room exploding with color—the entire basement was decorated with a huge array of flowers and balloons. Someone had found a string of old Christmas tree lights and made a heart on the wall. And instead of bearing the usual kettles of soup, the tables were laden with roast turkeys, mashed potatoes, cranberry sauce, and trimmings.

The street people asked what was going on. Terry explained, "My friend Patty, whom you know, has become my wife. And we thought—who more appropriate to share our celebration with than you, our friends."

That day over one hundred of Terry and Patty's friends from

the streets, as well as their families and other friends, participated in a joyous celebration. Afterward Patty invited guests to take the decorations with them. Every doily, flower, and bit of decoration was carefully wrapped up and sent home with delighted guests, who packed them away as souvenirs. Terry and Patty, like thousands of others, have discovered the secret of abundant living—that the good life of God is to be found in sharing life, not in seeking it.

Remember how the story of God ends? A wedding reception! Listen to Jesus as he tells a parable of those who are unwilling to relinquish their self-involved lives to be part of God's world-changing future.

> The kingdom of heaven may be compared to a king, who gave a wedding feast for his son. And he sent out his slaves to call those who had been invited to the wedding feast, and they were unwilling to come. Again he sent out other slaves saying, "Tell those who have been invited, 'Behold, I have prepared my dinner; my oxen and my fattened livestock are all butchered and everything is ready; come to the wedding feast.' " But they paid no attention and went their way, one to his own farm, another to his business, and the rest seized his slaves and mistreated them and killed them.
>
> But the king was enraged and sent his armies, and destroyed those murderers, and set their city on fire. Then he said to his slaves, "The wedding is ready, but those who were invited were not worthy. Go therefore to the main highways, and as many as you find there, invite to the wedding feast." And those slaves went out into the streets, and gathered together all they found, both evil and good; and the wedding hall was filled with dinner guests. (Matt. 22:2-10, NASB)

Clearly it isn't enough to believe in God, for even the devil believes. And it isn't enough to receive Christ into our hearts, as important as that is. We must realize that to have any part in God's final wedding celebration we need to repent of self-involved lives and egocentric faith and seek God's kingdom first.

As we place God's dream and loving purposes at the center of our lives and congregations, we will find creative new ways that God will use our lives to make a difference. Then and only then will we discover who we are called to be. We will discover the role God has for us to play in the divine, world-changing drama. We will discover a way of life more festive and satisfying than anything this world can offer. We will find a new way up.

Listen to the final description of the transcendent dream of God pictured for us in Revelation.

> And I saw a new heaven and a new earth; for the first heaven and the first earth passed away, and there is no longer any sea. And I saw the holy city, new Jerusalem, coming down out of heaven from God, made ready as a bride adorned for her husband. And I heard a loud voice from the throne, saying, "Behold, the tabernacle of God is among men, and He shall dwell among them, and they shall be His people, and God Himself shall be among them, and He shall wipe away every tear from their eyes; and there shall no longer be any death; there shall no longer be any mourning, or crying, or pain; the first things have passed away." And He who sits on the throne said, "Behold, I am making all things new." (Rev. 21:1-5, NASB)

Welcome to life exploding with possibilities! Welcome to the adventure of working with our Creator Lord to see all things made new! Welcome to the wedding feast of God!

LIFE LINKS

find a new way up...

get linked

to the purposes of God

God has placed our future right in your own hands. You have the creative opportunity to find imaginative new ways to link your life with the purposes of God. You have an opportunity to create a life you can truly love.

What are you waiting for? Get linked!

God is waiting to use your mustard seed to change the world . . . to help you discover a way of life with more meaning than you ever imagined . . . to use your life to make a difference for God's kingdom.

How To Use

A Guide for Study and Action

In my years of work with InterVarsity Christian Fellowship, my staff colleagues and I have used this material on campus and as part of a conference called "Discipleship After Campus." We developed the conference in response to the needs of graduating college seniors who had been active members of InterVarsity and now had to translate their campus experience into lifelong patterns of kingdom faith and lifestyle. The result has been a growing movement of our alumni into active partnerships in local congregations, church planting, ministry to the poor, and racial reconciliation.

I will try in the following pages to share strategies, ideas, and reflections that will help you use this book most effectively. Please read through the entire guide before you begin. Many of the ideas can be used for various chapters. Be sure to use the questions in the book at the end of each chapter and encourage people to use the "Life Line" summaries. Start each session with prayer and be creative.

For Leaders, Teachers, and Facilitators

If you are planning to lead a group through this book, or teach it in a Sunday school or other class, congratulations! You have made an excellent and challenging choice.

As you embark, be ready to live the book yourself. This is a book about how we live; therefore, a "study" of it must go beyond mere analysis and discussion (though these may serve as important components of the process) to trying things out as living options. Your leadership experience will be most fun and most beneficial if you take risks along the way.

Please help the students focus each chapter's discussion around the point of the chapter. If you do, you will see how the chapter fits together and help each of us create a life we can truly love.

Gather a Group

Live It Up! is written for God's people—in the plural! Find five or ten others in your congregation, on your campus, or in your community who are concerned about creating kingdom lives. Work together to discuss and apply the text. So much of this book is written with Christian community in mind that you will find yourself limited without partners. If you are studying in a large fellowship or class, consider breaking down to discussion-size small groups on a regular basis. It is important that everyone find and express ideas. You will be surprised at the creativity of some of your friends! The call is to create lives that do not conform to this world but rather bear the characteristics of the coming kingdom of God. Your nonconformity will put you in tension with systems and people around you, and it will be a great blessing to have the encouragement of fellow pilgrims on this journey.

Ideas for Action

Here are ways we have applied the issues and ideas in this book. Feel free to pick, choose, and create your own!

Chapter 1—Discovering Life

Point of the Chapter

The purpose of this chapter is to explore why our lives are so incredibly stressed yet so lacking in direction, purpose, and celebration.

Teaching the Chapter

In this session it will be important to enable participants to figure out why their lives are so stressed and their schedules so jammed. Here are ideas for helping the students grasp the point of the chapter.

1. Our lives are so busy! Sometimes we need to stop and look at what we are doing and figure out where our time is going. Ask your group to keep a time journal for one week. Suggest they write down each evening how they have used their time that day. When they bring their week's time journal back to the study group ask them to answer the following questions in writing in their time journals:

    a. Are you satisfied with the way you used your time in the past week? If no, explain why?
    b. Was your week more pressured than you cared for? Where is this pressure coming from?
    c. What does the way you used your time suggest are the most important areas of your life? What do you seem to value most?
    d. How might you change your use of time to create a way of life that is both less stressed and more fully reflects the things you really value most?

2. Rent the video "Lost in America," fix popcorn and watch it with your study group. After the video is over discuss these questions:

    a. Did you identify more with David or Linda?
    b. What did you think of their way of dealing with the stress-rate?

c. If you were to take radical action as portrayed in "Lost in America," to alter your entire way of life to find a new way up, how would you do it?

3. Watch an hour of network television together. Ask the class to take notes while watching both the programs and advertisements. Ask them to answer these questions:

a. What is being promoted as the "good life" in programs or advertisements? What do they seem to suggest is essential to living life up?

b. If you followed the notions of the good life promoted on TV, would you be able to live a less stressed, more satisfying way of life? Explain.

c. How does a biblical notion of the good life compare to what is being promoted on the TV programs you watched? Which do you feel most drawn to? Why?

Chapter 2—Discerning Half-truths and False Visions

Point of the Chapter

The purpose of this chapter is to enable us to discuss more fully the half-truths and false visions to which we have given our lives.

Teaching the Chapter

Your major task is to use the hypothetical couples in this chapter to help participants identify what the aspirations are that are driving their lives. What are their images of the better future?

1. Begin by asking four couples or four individuals to role play each of the four couples in chapter 2. After they are done role playing ask participants to discuss the following questions:

a. What are the different notions of the better future in each of those four models? Where do each of these ideas about the better future come from?

    b. Which of these different notions of the better future are closest to your views of the better future? Where do your views come from?

    c. What are some biblical images of the better future? How are they different from the images in the four models? How are they different from your own images?

2. Ask people to discuss if they were to seriously live toward biblical instead of cultural views of the better future. How might this help them create a less-stressed and a more meaningful way of life, a new way up?

Chapter 3—Connecting with the Story of God

Point of the Chapter

    The intent of this chapter is to enable you to relive the panoramic story of God in order to discover God's purposes for our lives and God's world to help you find a new way up.

Teaching the Chapter

    Many of us who have been committed to God for a long time have never been challenged to replace the aspirations of the culture in which we have been raised with the purposes of God.

1. Have your study group review all you have discussed to this point—
    a. Why are our lives more stressed and less meaningful than we long for?
    b. What is our image of the better future? To what aspirations are we giving our lives?
    c. How are God's purposes, expressed in the Story of God in chapter 3, different from the aspirations for which we have been laboring?

2. Have your study group read the following passages from the story of God:

Isaiah

| 65:17-19 | 58:5-7 | 2:1-4 |
| 35:1-7 | 25:6-9 | 9:2-7 |

Before they read, write up on a flip chart or blackboard a single question: "What seem to be God's purposes for the human future?" in these passages. Invite them to discuss their answer to this question in a small groups first. Then ask them to share their answers with the entire study group and list them on the flip chart. Ask them to meditate in silence on God's purposes for a few minutes and then perhaps sing "Seek Ye First the Kingdom of God."

Then ask them to discuss in small groups how God's purposes for the better future are different from the aspirations of the North American dream. Again have the small groups share their input with the entire group and list their input on the flip chart.

Next ask the study group to read aloud: Luke 4:17-21; 7:22-23. Before they read write at the top of the flip chart or blackboard a single question: "How did Jesus Christ relate his life to the purposes of God?" After they discuss the question in small groups write their responses to the whole group down on the flip chart. (Of course what happened is that Jesus made God's purposes his purposes. What it meant for Jesus to be the Messiah of God quite simply was to devote his life to working for the purposes of God.)

Finally ask participants to discuss in their small groups "How might your life be different if you put the others or purposes of God in place of the self-seeking aspirations of North American culture?" Again have the small groups share their responses with the entire group.

Chapter 4—Remembering Stories of Hope

Point of the Chapter

The purpose of this chapter is to help us find in the studies of those who have gone before us the courage to follow Christ today, to place the purposes of God in the very center of our lives. Then we too can find a way of life that truly counts.

Teaching the Chapter

In this chapter we take a remembering journey into the Christian past. And get to know men and women who put God's purposes first in their lives, often at a very dear cost. We specifically look at the difference their lives made.

1. Ask one or two of the students to read aloud their favorite story in this chapter. Then lead a discussion around these questions:
   a. What choices did people in this chapter make to place God's purposes first in their lives?
   b. How did their commitment to the purposes of God make a difference in the lives around them?
   c. In what ways have these stories challenged you to put God's purposes first?

2. Play the Saints Game. Give members of your study group a chance to get to know others who have gone before. Photo-copy biographies on as many saints as you have people in your class (from encyclopedias, church history books or books listing the saints). Tape a saint's biography on the back of each member of the study group as they come together. Then each person needs to ask others in the group questions to figure out what saint is taped on their back. Have a small prize for the person who guesses their saint first.

   Have all participants share what they learned about their saint, particularly the impact they had on the world around them as a result of placing God's purposes first in their lives.

   Finally, in prayer have people thank God for those who have gone before us, who have chosen to put first things first and made a difference in God's world.

Chapter 5—Choosing A Life That Counts

Point of the Chapter

The purpose of this chapter is to persuade you not only to commit your life to God but placing the purposes of God at the absolute center of your life. To find a new way up like those who have gone before us.

Teaching the Chapter

It's Showtime! This is the chapter in which it will be essential to give every participant an opportunity to commit their lives not only to God, but to the purposes of God to make God's world new.

1. *Check out the fields.* It's time to get out and see what God is doing in your community. Arrange ahead to take your study group into a community of need nearby. Urban or rural. Set up an appointment with a Christian ministry working within that community of need. When you return to your regular meeting place ask students—
   a. to describe the physical conditions of the community they visited,
   b. to describe the people they saw in the community. Both their strength and their struggles,
   c. to discuss the Christian ministry you visited and their effectiveness in oppressing the needs in the community,
   d. to explain how this experience has impacted their lives.

2. *Check out the ministry.* Have members of the study group identify and discuss ministries they are involved in each week beyond the doors of the church in their own communities. Ask the following questions:
   a. How did you get involved in your area of ministry?
   b. What has been the most satisfying part of your involvement?

3. *Check out the chapter.* Have people discuss the following questions in small groups and then share their input with the entire group:
   a. What would happen if all Christians who claimed to believe in God did the same thing Jesus and the first disciples did—reordered their lives around the purposes of God? What if we truly worked to give "sight to the blind, release to the captives, and good news to the poor"? What would happen if our ministry vocation became the orchestrating center of our lives and families?

And if every Christian took time to be involved in ministry every week?

b. How would you have to reorder your time style or your family's time style to have time to be involved in ministry every week?

c. Ask all members to use the "active listening process" in chapter 5. Have them share what they sense is God's ministry vocation for their lives and families. Ask what they need to do to actually place God's ministry purposes first in their lives. Finally ask when they plan to begin. Offer the study group as a support and accountability group to help get them underway. Write or call students during the week after they make the decision to put first things first to see. . . . To see how they are doing.

Chapter 6—Discovering A Life You Can Love

Point of the Chapter

The purpose of this chapter is to enable us to find a new to be in the world—a way of life that is a foretaste of the future of God.

Teaching the Chapter

The last chapter stressed the importance of doing (taking time every week to work for the purpose of God). This chapter emphasizes being. The author insists that the first call of the Gospel isn't to activity or ministry, as important as that is, but to being. In this chapter, then, the focus is on prayer, community, celebration, and recorded time styles and lifestyles.

1. *Redefining the good life and the better future.* See the section entitled "Whole-life discipleship: Biblically rediscovering a new way up." In this section the author outlines a Bible study through the gospel of Luke. Make four lists, two before the study, one during, and one after. Lead the study group in one session through very brief testing of this approach to biblical study.

What makes this study unique is that most Bible studies focus the application sincerely on spiritual and relationship areas. This study suggests goals that also challenge our fundamental values, the direction of our lives, and even our notions of what constitutes the "good life."

In having your study group work through this study of Luke, particularly have them discover what seem to be values important in Jesus' life and teachings. What seems to be Jesus' notion of the good life? How does it differ from our North American culture values and aspirations?

2. *Considering a new way of being in the world.* After you have done a quick study through Luke, ask each person in the study group to select a partner with whom to discuss a new way of being. Ask them to discuss the following questions:

   a. How would you characterize your prayer life? Where is it strong and growing? Where does it need help?

   b. Are you presently involved in a small group? If yes, what is the focus of the small group? Does it give you the support and accountability you need in your discipleship and ministry to others?

   c. Are you interested in moving from compartmentized to whole-life discipleship around God's kingdom purposes and kingdom values?

   d. Together with your partner, brainstorm ways you could reorder your timestyle and lifestyle to have more time and money to invest in things that matter. Also brainstorm ways you can add more celebration to your life.

Have each couple share with the entire group creative new ways they are considering moving into whole life discipleship.

Again offer the prayers, support and accountability of the entire group to each person who wants to take new ground.

Chapter 7—Sharing Life Beyond the Doors of Home and Church

Point of the Chapter

The purpose of this chapter is to enable local congregation to became more active and creative in sharing God's love beyond the doors of home and church.

Teaching the Chapter

Even as Christ was called to be a person for others we are called to be a people for others. The problem is that little of the total resources of North American churches gets directed outward to address the urgent and growing needs in our communities on God's world. You may remember the author stated that, in his experience, most churches spend at least 80 percent of their time and their money on themselves. The intent of this chapter is to challenge the North American church to be a church for others.

1. Ask each member of your study group to do an audit of their own local congregation to secure a rough estimate regarding how much time and money actually gets beyond the walls of the local church in mission to others. When they bring these rough audits to the study group, break them into small groups to discuss these questions:

   a. How much time and money is invested outside the local church to address the needs of others?

   b. Given the way the local congregation prioritize its use of time and money, what seems to be most important? Do you find these priorities and the values they reflect to be consistent with the values reflected in Scripture?

   c. What seems to be the operational vision of the congregation at this point? How might the local church be different if the leadership worked with the people to develop a stronger sense of focused biblical vision?

   d. What are some of the growing areas of human need in your community? What are creative new ways your church could direct resources outward to address these urgent needs?

Again have these small groups share their insights and ideas with the entire group. Suggest that members share their ideas with their pastors and bring the feedback to the next session.

2. Have each person in your group write a "future history" of what their local church would look like in ten years if they really decided to become a church for others. Particularly describe how this might affect the local community. Have them bring their future histories to class; have several of the more creative ones read aloud. You might invite pastors to sit in on this session and discuss with the group ways to sharpen the vision and direct more of the congregation outward in mission to the growing areas of need.

Chapter 8—Creating New Possibilities

Point of the Chapter

The intent of this chapter is to enable you to create new possibilities for your life and God's world—creating a way of life you can truly love.

Teaching the Chapter

This chapter invites every reader to burst the wineskin of conventional Christianity and find a spectrum of creative new ways to live life up. Encourage participants to set aside their fears and spend this entire session unleashing their creativity. It would be great if this final session could be in a home with nachos or other munchies to celebrate your final session together. It will be important for this session to have about thirty sheets of large newsprint and perhaps ten big felt tip markers.

1. Idea Storming—Creating a life you can love.

Look for the heading "Idea-storming—Creating a life you can love." In this section are seven creativity options. I suggest you add three more that are particularly pertinent to your study group. Then invite members to participate in the creativity group in which they are most interested in working on out of the ten options. Give each group two large sheets of newsprint and a felt tip marker. Challenge them to come up with some fresh new possibilities for their lives.

Allow about an hour and a half for the three phases of "idea storming." Have someone read the idea-storming section from the book before you begin so everyone understands what is expected. Ask them to list all ideas. Share their ideas, limit each group to two minutes (with applause) Holding their idea—storming sheets for others to see.

2. Building a bridge back home—after you are done sharing ask each person to spend some time silently and prayerfully writing down how they plan to act on some of their own creative new ideas. Ask them to list three immediate action steps. Then invite them to share what they plan to do with one other person. Ask them to exchange phone number and call one another in seven days to see how it's going.

Give those who want to the opportunity to share their plans action steps with the entire group. Conclude with a time of prayer for one another and for the new possibilities God is around.

Consider setting a study group reunion date within six weeks of the end of the class. Make it a time to celebrate and encourage those who are finding a new way up—who are making their lives count by putting God's purposes first in their lives, families, and congregation.

> —*Prepared in collaboration with Tom Sine*
> *by Allison Van Detta Stewert,*
> *co-director, Southern California*
> *InterVarsity.*

Notes

Start Here . . .
1. Louis Harris poll, *Inside America New York Vintage,* 1987, pp. 8-10.
2. Tom Sine, *Wild Hope* (Dallas: Word Books, 1991).
3. Tom Sine, *Mustard Seed Conspiracy,* (Dallas: Word Books, 1981).
4. Donald Kraybill, *The Upside-Down Kingdom,* rev. ed. (Scottdale, Pa.: Herald Press, 1991).

1. Discovering Life
1. Trina Paulia, *Hope for the Flowers* (Mahwah, N.J.: Paulist Press, 1978), pp. 21-94.
2. Erma Bombeck, *Aunt Erma's Cope Book* (New York: Fawcett Crest 1979), pp. 47-53.
3. "Special Report: They Live to Buy," *Newsweek,* 31 December 1984, p. 28.
4. Conrad M. Arensberg and Arthur N. Niehoff, "American Cultural Values" from James P. Spradley and Michael A. Rynkuwich, *The Nacirema: Readings on American Culture* (Boston: Little, Brown, 1975), p. 367.
5. Paul L. Wachtel, *The Poverty of Affluence: A Psychological Portrait of the American Way of Life* (New York: Free Press, 1983), p. 546.
6. Robert Anderson, *Stress Power: How to Turn Tension into Energy* 22 (New York: Human Sciences Press, 1978), 18.
7. *We Are Driven: The Compulsive Behavior America Applauds* (Nashville: Thomas Nelson, 1991), pp. 4–9.
8. Wachtel, p. 61.

9. Ibid., pp. 61-65.
10. Henri Nouwen, "Creating True Intimacy," *Sojourners,* June 1985, 15-16.
11. Nouwen, p. 15.

2. Discerning Half-truths and False Visions
1. Robert Cole, "Our Self-Centered Children—Heirs of the 'Me' Decade," *U.S. News and World Report,* 15 February 1981, p. 80.
2. Alexander W. Astin, "Student Values: Knowing More about Where We Are Today," American Association of Higher Education Bulletin, May 1984, pp. 10-12.
3. Robert Bellah, et al., *Habits of the Heart* (New York: Harper & Row, 1985), p. 6.
4. Daniel Yankelvoch, *New Rules: Searching for Self-Fulfillment in a World Turned Upside Down* (New York: Bamta, 1981).
5. Leslie Newbigin, "Cross Currents in Ecumenical and Evangelical Mission," *International Bulletin of Missionary Research,* October 1982, p. 149.
6. Gabriel Fackre, *The Religious Right and the Christian Faith* (Grand Rapids, Mich.: Eerdmans, 1982), p. 50.
7. Jerry Falwell, *Listen America* (New York: Doubleday, 1980), p. 25.
8. Mark A. Noll, Nathan O. Hatch, George M. Marsden, *In Search for Christian America* (Westchester, Ill.: Crossway Books, 1983), p. 17.
9. Robert Webber, *Church in the World* (Grand Rapids, Mich.: Zondervan, 1986), p. 226.

3. Connecting with the Story of God
1. Garrison Keillor, *Lake Wobegon Days* (New York: Viking, 1985), pp. 276-279.
2. Robert McAfee Brown, "Starting Over: New Beginning Points for Theology," *Christian Century,* 14 May 1980, pp. 547-548.
3. Christopher J. H. Wright, "The Use of the Bible in Social Ethics: Paradigms, Type, and Eschatology," *Transformation,* January-March 1984, p. 11.
4. John S. Dunne, *A Search for God in Time and Memory: An Exploration Traced in the Lives of Individuals from Augustine to Sartre* (London: Macmillan, 1969), p. 7.
5. Christopher Wright, 12.
6. Walter Brueggemann, *The Land* (Philadelphia: Fortress Press, 1977), 18.
7. Frederick Buechner, *Telling the Truth: The Gospel as Tragedy, Comedy and Fairy Tale* (New York: Harper & Row, 1977), pp. 45-53.
8. Brueggemann, 43.
9. David J. Bosch, *Witness to the World* (Atlanta: John Knox Press, 1980), p. 209.

10. Jürgen Möltmann, *The Crucified God: The Cross of Christ as the Foundation and Criticism of Christian Theology* (San Francisco: Harper & Row, 1974), p. 216.
11. Irving Fineman, "The Wedding in Misinetz" in Philip and Hanna Goodman, *The Jewish Marriage Anthology* (Philadelphia: The Jewish Publication Society, 1967), pp. 137-139.
12. Howard Snyder, *A Kingdom Manifesto* (Downers Grove, Ill.: Inter-Varsity Press, 1985) p. 33.

4. Remembering Stories of Hope
 1. Based on Herbert Thurston and Donald Attwater, eds., *Butler's Lives of the Saints,* vol. 1 (New York: P. J. Kenedy and Sons, 1956), pp. 26-27.
 2. Based on Adoman, *Life of Columba* (London: Thomas Nelson, 1961).
 3. Based on *Butler's Lives of the Saints,* vol. 1, pp. 397-398.
 4. Myron Augsburger, *Faithful Unto Death; Fifteen Young People Who Were Not Afraid to Die for Their Faith* (Waco, Tex.: Word Books, 1975), pp. 85-91.
 5. Elliot Wright, *Holy Company: Christian Heroes and Heroines* (New York: Macmillan Press, 1980), pp. 120-123.
 6. Ibid., p. 9.
 7. Donald W. Dayton, *Discovering an Evangelical Heritage* (New York: Harper & Row, 1976), p. 12.
 8. Ibid., p. 12.
 9. Ibid., p. 10.

5. Choosing a Life That Counts
 1. James W. Fowler, *Becoming Adult, Becoming Christian: Adult Development and Christian Faith* (New York: Harper & Row, 1984), p. 93.

6. Discovering a Life You Can Love
 1. John Alexander, "Why We Must Ignore Jesus," *The Other Side,* October 1977, p. 8.
 2. Donald B. Kraybill, *The Upside-Down Kingdom,* rev. ed. (Scottdale, Pa.: Herald Press, 1990).
 3. Quoted in Jim Wallis, *The Call to Conversion; Recovering the Gospel for These Times* (San Francisco: Harper & Row, 1981), p. 15.
 4. Quoted in Henri Nouwen, *Reaching Out* (New York: Doubleday, 1975), p. 89.
 5. Ibid.

7. Sharing Life Beyond the Doors of Home and Church
 1. Ray Bakke, a Christian urbanologist who works for the Lausanne Commission, does a fine job of helping people understand their

cities. He has helped Christian leaders from Manila to Chicago learn what makes their community tick and how to identify arenas for Christian mission response. His videotape, "The City for God's Sake" is available from World Vision, 919 W. Huntington Drive, Monrovia, CA 91016.

2. Dietrich Bonhoeffer, *The Cost of Discipleship* (New York: Macmillan, 1963), p. 225.
3. Lausanne Committee for World Evangelization, *The Lausanne Covenant,* Lausanne Occasional Papers No. 3 (Minneapolis: World Wide Publications, 1975), p. 15.
4. *Consultation on the Relationship Between Evangelism and Social Responsibility,* a report from CRESR 82 (Grand Rapids, Mich.: Reformed Bible School, 1982), 15.
5. "Social Transformation: The Church in Response to Human Need," statement issued from the Wheaton 83 conference, sponsored by World Evangelical Fellowship, Wheaton, Ill., 1983.
6. Wayne Bragg, "Social Transformation," in *Christian Response to Human Need,* ed. Tom Sine (Monrovia, Calif.: Missions Advanced Research & Communication Center, 1983).
7. World Concern's address is Box 33,000, Seattle, WA 98133.
8. "Claiming Turf in Hispanic Chicago," *Eternity,* June 1984, p. 25.
9. Ibid.
10. Gordon Cosby, *Handbook for Mission Groups* (Washington, D.C.: Church of the Saviour), pp. 2-9.
11. Rene Laurentin, *Miracle in El Paso* (Ann Arbor, Mich.: Servant Publications, 1982), p. 14.
12. "In Christ, Reconciliation," *Jubilee International: A Newsletter of Prison Fellowship International,* July-September 1983, pp. 4-5.
13. John R. Stott, *Involvement, Vol. 1: Being a Responsible Christian in a Non-Christian Society* (Old Tappan, N.J.: Fleming H. Revell, 1985); Donald B. Kraybill, *The Upside-Down Kingdom,* rev. ed. (Scottdale, Pa.: Herald Press, 1990).
14. John Shea, *Stories of Faith,* (Chicago: Thomas More Press, 1980), pp. 200-301.

8. Creating New Possibilities
1. Harold Best, "God's Creation and Human Creativity" (unpublished paper, Wheaton College, 1983), p. 8.
2. Emil Brunner, *Christianity and Civilization* (New York: Charles Scribner's Sons, 1948), p. 157.
3. Harvey Cox, *Feast of Fools: A Theological Essay on Festivity and Fantasy* (Cambridge, Mass.: Harvard University Press, 1969), pp. 9-10.
4. John Naisbitt and Patricia Aburdene, *Re-Inventing the Corporation* (New York: Warner Books, 1985), p. 67.
5. Roger Von Oech, *A Kick in the Seat of the Pants* (New York: Harper & Row, 1986), p. 31.

6. Ibid., p. 60.
7. Bruce Skagen, San Francisco *Chronicle,* 13 May 1984.
8. If you actually implement your creative ideas, I would like to hear about it. Or if you know of anyone involved in creative new approaches to lifestyle change, celebration, community, or mission, please drop me a note at Box 45867, Seattle, WA 98145. We are developing a computer file on Christian innovation to share with the larger church, and we want to include models you are creating or are in touch with.
9. Joetta Handrich Schlabach with Kristina Mast Burnett, *Extending the Table: A World Community Cookbook* (Scottdale, Pa.: Herald Press, 1991).
10. "How the Ngozis Changed," *The Commission* (magazine of the Foreign Misison Board of the Southern Baptist Convention), December 1984, pp. 55-59.
11. Elizabeth O'Connor, *Eighth Day of Creation* (Waco, Tex.: Word Books, 1971), p. 17.

Begin Now
1. John H. Westerhoff III, *Inner Growth Outer Change: An Educational Guide to Church Renewal* (New York: The Seabury Press, 1979) p. 135.

The Author

Tom Sine is a futurist by profession. He works in the areas of futures research and planning with major denominations and Christian organizations such as World Concern, where he has been a staff member and consultant for over ten years. He is also the director of Mustard Seed Associates. He is a prolific writer whose articles have appeared in periodicals ranging from *Sojourners* to *Christianity Today*. His book, *The Mustard Seed Conspiracy* (1981) won several awards and became a Christian bestseller. In 1991 he authored a book on the future of the church entitled *Wild Hope*.

A Presbyterian layman, Tom works with a broad spectrum of denominations. He is in wide demand as a speaker and served as coordinator for Wheaton '83, an international conference which gave the original impetus for this book. In addition to his speaking, writing, and consultation work, Tom holds creativity workshops for churches and other Christian groups.

Tom holds a Ph.D. in American history from the University of Washington and has served on the faculty of the University of Washington, Seattle Pacific University, and Fuller Theological Seminary. He has lectured widely at a number of colleges and seminaries, including Wheaton College and Eastern Mennonite College.

Tom's two sons, Wes and Clint Sine, also live in Seattle, as does his mother Katherine. Tom is married to Christine Aroney Sine, who has worked as a physician in international health care. They attend two churches in Seattle, Evergreen Mennonite and St. Lukes Episcopal.

For additional information about Mustard Seed Associates, issues raised in this book, or Tom or Christine's availability, write Mustard Seed Associates, P.O. Box 45867, Seattle, WA 98145.